CodeNotes® for J#

Edited by GREGORY BRILL

CodeNotes® for J#

RANDOM
HOUSE

NEW YORK

A Random House Trade Paperback Original

Copyright © 2003 by Infusion Development Corporation

All rights reserved under International and Pan-American Copyright Conventions. Published in the United States by Random House, an imprint of The Random House Publishing Group, a division of Random House, Inc., New York, and simultaneously in Canada by Random House of Canada Limited, Toronto.

RANDOM HOUSE TRADE PAPERBACKS and colophon are trademarks of Random House, Inc.

CodeNotes is a registered trademark of Infusion Development Corporation.

Microsoft, Windows, Windows 2000, .NET, VB.NET, C#, J#, ASP.NET, Internet Information Server, and Internet Explorer are trademarks of Microsoft Corporation.

Java, JDK, JRE, J2EE, and all Java-based trademarks are trademarks or registered trademarks of Sun Microsystems.

Library of Congress Cataloging-in-Publication Data
Codenotes for J# / edited by Gregory Brill.
p.   cm.
ISBN 0-8129-7156-6 (pbk.)
1. J# (Computer program language)   I. Brill, Gregory.
QA76.73.J2C63 2003   005.13'3—dc21   2003047068

Printed in the United States of America
Random House website address: www.atrandom.com

2 4 6 8 9 7 5 3 1

First Edition

Using CodeNotes

PHILOSOPHY

The CodeNotes philosophy is that the core concepts of any technology can be presented succinctly. The product of many years of consulting and training experience, the CodeNotes series is designed to make you productive in a technology in as short a time as possible.

CODENOTES POINTERS

Throughout the book, you will encounter CodeNotes pointers: JS010101. Notice that the first two letters are J and S (as in Jay Sharp) and the remaining characters are numbers. These pointers are links to additional content available online at the CodeNotes website. To use a CodeNotes pointer, simply point a Web browser to www.codenotes.com and enter the pointer number. The website will direct you to an article or an example that provides additional information about the topic.

CODENOTES STYLE

The CodeNotes series follows certain style guidelines:

- Code objects and code keywords are highlighted using a special font. For example: `array[3]`.

- Code blocks, screen output, and command lines are placed in individual blocks with a special font:

```
//This is an example code block
```

Listing ChapterNumber.ListingNumber Some code

WHAT YOU NEED TO KNOW BEFORE CONTINUING

This book is geared toward developers who are familiar with, or are in the process of learning, basic Java language syntax. Although we provide a refresher on basic syntax in Chapter 3, many of the examples in this book assume you have a working knowledge of Java language fundamentals, creating and compiling class files, basic language structure, the Collections Framework, and I/O classes. If you would like a quick refresher on these topics, or you are new to the Java language, you should consult *CodeNotes for Java* and *CodeNotes for J2EE*.

About the Authors

CRAIG WILLS is a technical writer for Infusion Development Corporation. He has worked in technical documentation at a variety of institutions in both Canada and the United States, including major banks, Internet consulting firms, and software component developers. Craig is the primary author of *CodeNotes for Web Services* and a coauthor of *CodeNotes for XML* and *CodeNotes for Web-Based UI.* He currently lives in Bowling Green, Ohio.

ROBERT MCGOVERN works as a consultant, architect, and trainer for Infusion Development Corporation. He has worked on everything from large mortgage and stock-trading systems to biomechanics data-collection and analysis systems. Rob currently lives in Ohio with his wife and their cat. Rob was primary author on *CodeNotes for J2EE, CodeNotes for Java,* and *CodeNotes for Oracle 9i,* and coauthor on *CodeNotes for ASP.NET* and *CodeNotes for Web Services in Java and .NET.*

CONTRIBUTING AUTHOR

SHELDON FERNANDEZ is a senior developer at Infusion Development Canada, located in Toronto, Canada. He has developed software for Silicon Valley start-ups, as well as financial and medical institutions in the United States and Canada. He has worked with Microsoft technology for many years and has taught numerous aspects of the .NET Framework (including C#) to a variety of companies, including financial institutions in New York City and software companies in California. Sheldon is also primary author on *CodeNotes for C#, CodeNotes for ASP.NET, CodeNotes for VB.NET,* and *CodeNotes for .NET.*

ABOUT THE EDITOR

GREGORY BRILL is the founder and president of Infusion Development Corporation, a firm specializing in architecting global securities trading and analytic systems for some of the world's largest investment banks. Gregory is the author of *Applying COM+,* and has written and been quoted in a variety of technology user and business articles. He lives in the New York metro area with his wife and young daughter.

ABOUT INFUSION DEVELOPMENT

Infusion Development Corporation (www.infusiondev.com) is a technology training, software development, and consulting company specializing in the financial services industry. Based in Lower Manhattan, with offices in Toronto, Canada, and Bangalore, India, Infusion Development created the CodeNotes book series.

More information about the authors and Infusion Development Corporation can be found at www.codenotes.com/do/aboutus.

Acknowledgments

First, I'd like to thank Mary Bahr, our unflappable editor at Random House, who paved the way for the CodeNotes series. I'd also like to thank the production, sales, and business teams at Random House, with particular thanks to Richard Elman. Next, I'd like to thank the folks from Microsoft who helped make this book a reality, in particular, Morris Sim and Janie Schwark, who convinced us of the need for this book. In addition, Brian Keller and Mythreyee Ganapathy provided invaluable technical and editorial assistance. Many thanks also to the Advanced Placement College Board for providing Microsoft with assistance for creating a Visual J# .NET implementation of the Marine Biology Simulation Case Study used in the Advanced Placement Computer Science courses. Finally, I'd like to thank the J# Product Team for technical guidance with the book, and for producing a product that helps bridge the gap for Java developers wanting to move into the world of .NET development.

On the Infusion Development side, thank you to Tom Nicholson for his editorial efforts and the CodeNotes reviewers, who gave us invaluable feedback and suggestions on our early drafts. And thank you to the entire cast and crew of Infusion Development who have supported and encouraged this venture throughout, with special gratitude to Alim Somani, Irene Wilk-Dominique, and DeBorah Johnson, who helped administrate and manage so much of this process. I know CodeNotes was extremely trying and tough to do, and involved an awesome amount of research, writing, and editing. But here it is . . . exactly as we envisioned it.

—Gregory Brill

Contents

CodeNotes® for J#

Chapter 1

—

INTRODUCTION

The Java language is an extremely popular, object-oriented programming language originally released by Sun Microsystems in 1995. Over the past eight years, its user base (and fan base) has grown steadily due to its simplicity and robustness, and it can be found everywhere from professional software development companies to businesses to high school and college classrooms.

With the release of .NET, Microsoft's new framework for Windows software development, Microsoft has created an opportunity for Java developers to use the language they know and yet take full advantage of the Microsoft Visual Studio .NET Integrated Development Environment (VS .NET), which we will discuss later in this chapter. For the moment, you can think of Visual Studio .NET as a language-neutral development environment that assists you in writing code in any one of a number of languages. Regardless of the language you choose, VS .NET will ultimately compile your code into a universal language called Microsoft Intermediate Language (MSIL). MSIL is very similar in principle to Java bytecode. However, MSIL has additional benefits in terms of cross-language development.

J# (pronounced *jay-sharp*) is the newest language to be supported by the Visual Studio .NET environment and is essentially Java for the .NET Framework. Not only does J# allow Java developers to program comfortably within the Microsoft integrated development environment (IDE), it also allows them to take full advantage of the extensive libraries and capabilities inherent in the .NET Framework. Like any .NET language, J# can be used to write ASP.NET Web Applications (Active Server Pages .NET, covered in Chapter 5) applications, XML Web Services (Chapter 6), ADO.NET data applications (Chapter 8), and a host of other .NET target types. Keep in mind that the J# compiler understands the Java language, but ultimately compiles it to MSIL (instead of the bytecode you may be used to). Thus, the front end is Java, but the compiled results run on the Microsoft .NET Framework, as opposed to a Java Virtual Machine (JVM). We will look at the similarities and differences between the Java language and the .NET Framework later in this chapter.

In this book we will look at how you, as a Java developer, can take advantage of J# and Visual Studio .NET to create Windows and Web Applications quickly. We will begin by examining the basics of the J# language. If you already know Java, these basics will be completely familiar. We will then examine how you can design graphical user interfaces (GUIs) for your applications using Windows Forms and controls. We will also look at how J# can be used with ASP.NET to develop Web Applications and .NET Web Services, which allow two applications to communicate with one another over the Internet using language-neutral protocols. Finally, we will apply what we have learned in this book to a major case study currently used in the Advanced Placement (AP) Computer Science Program common to many high schools (Chapter 7), and show how a traditional Java application can be extended using the features of Visual Studio .NET.

Please remember that this book is not intended as an introduction to the Java programming language, although we will briefly review the basics in Chapter 3. For the most part, we will assume that the reader has at least some knowledge of basic Java syntax and structure, and some experience in standard programming practices.

J# Is the Java Language

The first question an experienced developer might ask is: Is J# really Java? The answer depends on how you define "Java." *Java* is a term that is applied to several technologies. The word *Java* can be used to describe a programming language, the class libraries that make up the development platform, and the runtime environment. J# *is based on* the Java language, so the syntax is immediately familiar to anybody who has written a Java program. J# also provides for some of the class library functionality found in Java, with support for the functionality of most of the JDK 1.1.4 classes, plus a few additional classes (such as collections) from JDK 1.2 (and higher). At face value this may seem like a somewhat outdated level of library functionality, however one must consider that in addition to addressing the most important JDK functionality, J# has *full access* to the .NET Framework and can easily incorporate any of the classes and functions found throughout the .NET Framework. So in many ways, by choosing to develop with J#, a Java developer gets the best of both worlds—a Java language and basic JDK functionality that is comfortable, and the ability to fully harness the power of the .NET Framework and Visual Studio .NET. Finally, J# runs within the context of the Common Language Runtime (more on this later) and not the Java Runtime Environment, but this is of little consequence when comparing the types of applications that one can create.

J# USES ENTIRELY JAVA SYNTAX

Almost any application you can develop in Java using the core Java libraries (java.lang, java.text, etc.) will compile and run as J#. This means that if you have the Java Developer's Kit (JDK) 1.1.4 or earlier from Sun, almost all of the classes (we'll cover some exceptions in Chapter 3) that fall under the java.* packages will run under the .NET Framework using identical syntax. For example, consider the very simple Java application in Listing 1.1.

```
public class HelloWorld
{
  public static void main(String args[])
  {
    System.out.println("Hello, world!");
  }
}
```

Listing 1.1 HelloWorld.java

You can compile this application in the traditional way, using javac.exe, the Java compiler from Sun, as shown in Listing 1.2.

```
javac HelloWorld.java
```

Listing 1.2 Compiling a traditional Java application

Running the application using java HelloWorld will produce the message "Hello, World!" on your console. Just as you compiled the application using javac.exe, however, you can also compile and run this application using the J# compiler. This can be done in two different ways. One way is to open a Visual Studio .NET Command Prompt (a command prompt with special settings so that it knows the paths of VS .NET tools) and use `vjc.exe`, the Visual J# command-line compiler, as in Listing 1.3. This program can be used in much the same way as `javac.exe`.

```
vjc HelloWorld.java
```

Listing 1.3 Compiling with Visual J#

However, instead of producing a `.class` file, this will create an `.exe` (executable) file that you can run simply by typing `HelloWorld`. This compiled executable will actually run on any Windows machine, as long as the system has the .NET Framework installed. Although you might think the .NET Framework exists only for Windows, there are actually several advanced initiatives to port the framework to other operating systems, including Linux and FreeBSD Unix (●CN🡒JS010004).

Another, perhaps better, way of compiling a J# application is to use Visual Studio to create a new project and add `HelloWorld.java` to the project. This will allow you to run it from within the IDE, and, if you want a GUI, you can easily extend your app to add Windows Forms using Visual Studio's Windows Form Designer (WFD). We won't explore this just yet—we'll get into the Forms Designer in Chapter 4.

In summary, J# supports the complete Java syntax for J2SE 1.1.4 of the Java specification, plus some extras such as collections. In addition, J# can also leverage the full .NET class library, which contains a tremendous variety of additional classes and is covered in Chapter 3.

J# DOESN'T USE A JAVA VIRTUAL MACHINE

A Java Virtual Machine (JVM) interprets compiled Java classes (`.class` files) and compiles them into native code for the operating system (OS) on which a given VM is running. This is how Java programs are able to run anywhere, on any given machine. Java code is traditionally compiled to bytecode using a compiler (`javac.exe`), and the bytecode can then be run on any system that has a JVM installed. Note that each OS platform needs to have its own JVM designed to process bytecode into instructions and machine code that is understandable to that particular platform. All JVMs are implementations of Sun's Java Virtual Machine specification (●CN🡒JS010005).

In contrast to Java, J# is neither compiled to bytecode, nor does it use a JVM to interpret compiled classes. However, the .NET methodology of J#

compilation and execution is quite similar: compilers for any .NET language, of which J# is only one, transform source code into a pseudo–assembly language called Microsoft Intermediate Language (MSIL, or IL for short). If you are interested in seeing IL code, you can actually use a special tool called ILDASM.EXE to decompile your assembly and examine MSIL directly (see ⌐▷JS010001 for details). For most purposes, however, you can think of IL and Java bytecode as performing the same functions. That is, you compile your source code into an intermediate form (IL for .NET, bytecode for Java) that must be interpreted by some sort of execution engine or virtual machine in order to run.

Compiled .NET applications will take the form of a dynamically linked library (DLL) or executable (EXE) file. It is important to note, however, that while .NET applications have DLL and EXE extensions, they are not really traditional Windows EXE or DLL files. The .NET versions are really just files that contain IL. So, instead of calling these files DLLs or EXEs, both types are generally called .NET *assemblies*.

When an assembly is executed, .NET uses an execution system called the Common Language Runtime (CLR) to convert the IL code into machine instructions. We'll take a closer look at the CLR later in this chapter. For now, you can think of it as being similar in function to a JVM; it is responsible for compiling IL into machine code for a specific operating system, taking into account the specifics of the platform on which an application is running to ensure compatibility.

Although the J# language specification was developed completely independently of Sun's Java specification, Microsoft has been very careful to ensure that Java code can be compiled using a J# compiler without any changes being necessary. So, in essence, J# *is* simply Java from a developer's perspective. Even though J# is not handled the same way as Java behind the scenes, those details are hidden from the developer.

J# DOESN'T INCLUDE J2EE SUPPORT

J# supports the J2SE 1.1.4 but does not support any of the additional technologies found in the Java 2 Enterprise Edition (J2EE) framework. J2EE is a secondary Java framework that is used for large-scale development projects and contains an entirely separate suite of technologies (see Table 1.1) from the J2SE.

If you are new to Java or are simply interested in the parts of Java included in the AP Computer Science course, the lack of support for J2EE should not immediately be an issue to you. However, more experienced Java developers may be concerned that some of the technologies with which they are familiar will no longer be accessible if they switch over to J#. Fortunately, every J2EE technology has an analogous feature in .NET that can be used to accomplish the same thing (and, in many cases, offers significant functional enhancements). Table 1.1 shows a brief comparative listing of some of the more popular J2EE technologies and their .NET counterparts.

Technology	J2EE Version	.NET Version
Database access	JDBC	ADO.NET
Dynamic Web pages	Servlets and JavaServer Pages (JSP)	Active Server Pages .NET (ASP.NET)
E-mail	JavaMail	System.Web.Mail namespace
Messaging	Java Messaging Service (JMS)	.NET Messaging
Middle-tier components	Enterprise JavaBeans (EJB)	.NET Managed Components
Naming and directory services	Java Naming and Directory Interface (JNDI)	System.DirectoryServices namespace
Remoting	Remote Method Invocation (RMI)	.NET Remoting
Transactions	Java Transaction API (JTA)	Microsoft Transaction Server (MTS)

Table 1.1 Comparison of J2EE and .NET technologies

Please note that in the latest versions of Java (JDK 1.4 and later), JDBC, RMI, and JNDI have all been moved to the Standard Edition but are still not included as part of J# (remember, J# supports 1.1.4 and earlier). For more information on J2EE technologies and their .NET equivalents, we recommend the books *CodeNotes for J2EE* and *CodeNotes for .NET*, respectively.

What Is the .NET Framework?

J# is simply one of several languages that can be compiled to MSIL and run under a larger encompassing entity—Microsoft's .NET Framework.

Depending upon your interests and development background, you may already have a number of ideas as to what the .NET Framework entails. This book will show that

- .NET fundamentally changes the manner in which most applications execute under the Windows operating system. With .NET, Microsoft has evolved from its traditional stance, favoring compiled components, and embraces virtual machine (VM) technology, which Java also draws from.
- .NET is essentially a language-neutral platform—the only actual language its underlying engine understands is MSIL. However, Microsoft and other vendors have created several dozen compilers that allow a wide variety of independent languages to be compiled into IL. (See ᵒᶜᴺJS010006 for a complete list.) This means that a developer can program in any or all of these languages and have the components work together seamlessly.
- In addition to introducing MSIL compilers for two new languages (J# and C#), .NET brings about significant extensions to Visual Basic and Visual C++, both of which can now be compiled to MSIL. .NET also provides a common library for all languages (discussed subsequently). This means that any functionality available to one language is available to every other, and even cross-language inheritance is possible (e.g., you can write a component in C# and inherit from its classes in J#, or vice versa!).
- .NET is built from the ground up with the Internet in mind, and embraces open Internet standards such as XML (eXtensible Markup Language) and HTTP (Hypertext Transfer Protocol). XML is also used throughout the Framework as a messaging instrument and for holding configuration information.

We will take a closer look at the .NET Framework in the sections that follow. However, for an even more thorough introduction, please see *CodeNotes for .NET*.

THE COMMON LANGUAGE RUNTIME

The Common Language Runtime (CLR) is the execution engine for all programs in the .NET Framework. The CLR is similar to a Java Virtual Machine. It executes and compiles MSIL code on the fly (just as the JVM does with bytecode), while simultaneously providing services such as garbage collection and exception handling. As mentioned previously, the J# compiler does not translate source code into native machine code, but converts it into IL code, which is, in turn, converted into machine code and run by the CLR through a process called JIT (just-in-time) compilation. Therefore, J# applications are said to be *managed* by the CLR. In .NET, code that executes within the CLR is referred to as *managed code* because it is controlled by the runtime. Code that executes outside the CLR boundaries (such as older VB6 and Win32 applications) is called *unmanaged code,* because it operates outside the control of the CLR.

THE BASE CLASS LIBRARY

Like all .NET languages, J# draws on functionality exposed through a collection of classes called the Base Class Library (BCL). The BCL provides thousands of prewritten classes that you can leverage for services such as file input/output and common operations such as sorting collections of data.

Consider, for example, how you currently manipulate a string. Recall that in traditional Java, you would use the String or StringBuffer classes found in the Java class libraries, which are part of the J2SE (e.g., java.lang.String or java.lang.StringBuffer). However, in J# you manipulate strings by using the System.String and System.StringBuilder classes found in the BCL. These classes will function almost exactly like the Java classes you are used to. In fact, Java users will find the BCL very similar to the Java class libraries in that the BCL contains classes that mirror the functionality of all the commonly used Java classes. BCL classes either will have the same name as familiar Java classes or will have aliases with Java class names that allow Java code to be compiled using the J# compiler. For example, System.StringBuffer automatically maps to StringBuilder.

The BCL is significant because it is accessible to *any* language that targets the CLR (not just J#). Thus, once you understand how to use the System.String class from the BCL, you can leverage it not only from J# but from *any* of the .NET languages.

J# COMPILER TOOLS

Writing .NET applications requires a compiler that translates source code into IL code. There are two ways to perform the compilation process in J#.

- Using the J# command-line compiler (vjc.exe) that ships with the .NET Framework. The command-line compiler allows you to write J# code in a text editor (Notepad, for example) and then produce a .NET program from the command prompt.
- Using Microsoft's latest integrated development environment (IDE)—Visual Studio .NET (VS .NET). VS .NET is a development tool that, among many other things, allows you to design GUIs and the code that supports them in several of the languages supported by .NET's compilers. VS .NET offers many sophisticated features such as automatic code generation and powerful debugging capabilities across multiple languages, both of which will be discussed in the next section of this chapter.

In general, you will want to use VS .NET for J# development. As we will see, for certain operations the IDE generates a considerable amount of boilerplate code behind the scenes (which you would otherwise have to write manually if you developed outside the tool). However, unlike the command-line compiler that ships with the .NET Framework (which is available from Microsoft for free), Visual Studio .NET must be purchased separately.

In addition to language compilers, the .NET Framework contains a large assortment of command-line utilities. Some of these utilities are incorporated directly into VS .NET's development environment, whereas others are exclusively stand-alone. We will examine some of these utilities throughout this book.

THE .NET LANGUAGES

In addition to J#, Microsoft provides four other language compilers for the .NET Framework:

- Visual Basic .NET, the new version of Visual Basic
- JScript .NET, an evolved version of the popular scripting tool
- C#, a brand-new language combining features of both Java and C++
- Managed C++, an enhanced version of C++

The first three compilers ship as part of the Framework (and thus are free); the fourth is included with VS .NET. Many companies are in the process of porting additional languages to the .NET Framework. Two noteworthy examples are NetCOBOL for VS .NET, by Fujitsu Software, and Visual Perl, by Active State (see ⌐**CN**⌐JS010006).

What Is Visual Studio .NET?

Visual Studio .NET is Microsoft's latest interactive development environment for designing console applications (discussed in Chapter 3), class libraries (Chapter 3), Windows desktop applications (Chapter 4), Web-based applications (Chapter 5), and a good deal more. The ".NET" part of the title stems from Microsoft's new emphasis on online technologies as the way of the future. Internet data sharing using XML Web Services (Chapter 6) is the key feature and a critical development in the information technology industry. Fortunately, Web Service systems are easily created with the VS .NET environment. In this section, we will look at just a few key features of VS .NET: the solution/project system, the IDE, the debugger, and the dynamic help system.

THE PROJECT SYSTEM

Visual Studio .NET organizes your workspace into solutions and projects. You can see the solutions and projects you currently have open in the Solution Explorer, which is typically located in the top right corner of the screen (Figure 1.1).

- A *solution* represents a group of projects defined within a file with the extension .sln. The primary purpose of a solution is to keep a related group of applications (or projects) together and to allow you to control the order in which projects get compiled into an application. Solution configuration will also allow you to establish dependencies between projects—again, this controls build order, as it ensures that the dependent projects will not be compiled before the projects they depend on.
- A *project* is a container that contains all of the code and configuration files for a single .NET assembly. An *assembly* can be either a DLL (dynamically linked library) or an EXE (executable). J# project information is contained within a file with the extension .vjsproj. You can have multiple projects in a single solution, but each one will be compiled to a separate assembly.

When you open Visual Studio .NET and you want to create a new application (in any language), the first thing you will do is click on the **New Project** button. You will then be presented with a window that allows you to choose from a wide variety of project templates. A *template*

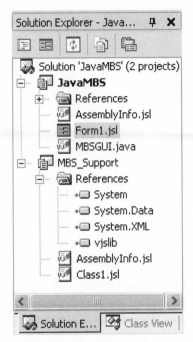

Figure 1.1 The Solution Explorer

is a set of pregenerated code that will allow you to start a new project of a particular type without having to create a lot of the generic background code yourself.

For example, if you create a new ASP.NET project using the ASP.NET Web Application template, Visual Studio will automatically create configuration files (Web.config and Global.asax; more on these in Chapter 5), a J# file containing assembly information (Assembly-Info.jsl), and a list of references to necessary namespaces in the BCL that contain built-in classes for developing Web Applications. Namespaces are essentially containers for classes. We will cover namespaces in Chapter 3. In addition to these files, VS .NET will create a new Web Form file, named WebForm1.aspx, with all the necessary classes and methods, so you can start building your application right away.

In this book, we will work exclusively with the J# set of templates, as shown in Figure 1.2. Specifically, we will look at four types of projects, three of which are pictured in Figure 1.2: console applications (Chapter 3), Windows applications (Chapter 4), ASP.NET Web Applications (Chapter 5), and ASP.NET Web Services (Chapter 6).

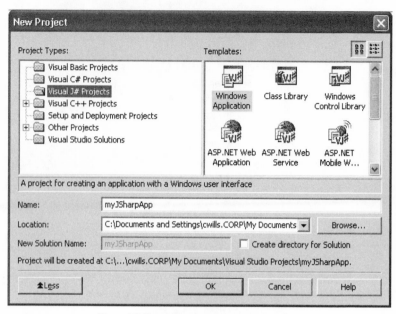

Figure 1.2 Creating a new project using templates

IDE OVERVIEW

The Visual Studio .NET Integrated Development Environment is the culmination of Microsoft's many years of IDE experience. It was influenced by many older languages such as Visual Basic, Visual C++, and Visual Interdev (an ASP Web development IDE). The latest version of VS .NET by default ships with and supports four major programming languages (J#, C#, VB.NET, and C++) from a single user interface. VS .NET further supports a variety of project types (represented by templates, as shown in Figure 1.2) in each of these languages, ranging from simple Windows applications to full-fledged interactive online projects. Because it is extensible, other languages can plug in to VS .NET, allowing you to use VS .NET to program in a much wider array of languages.

The IDE itself is completely customizable—you can maximize, minimize, and move around its various components to make the development experience more comfortable to you. However, the default organization provides access to all the components you will need when starting out with Visual Studio for the first time, in a generically convenient layout. Figure 1.3 shows the default IDE setup.

Let's take a closer look at the five parts of the screen labeled in Figure 1.3:

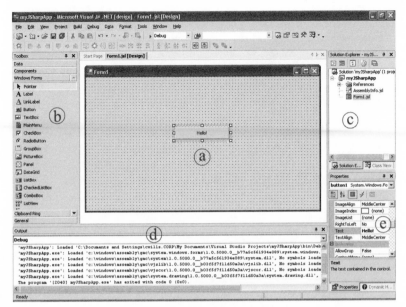

Figure 1.3 Default Visual Studio layout

The Main Window (a)

The main window is actually a container for several types of other documents. In this area, you may see code views, form designer windows, XML documents, or any other type of document you open in VS .NET. In Figure 1.3, the main work area is showing a form Design window. This window is part of the form designer and helps you paint your user interface by dragging controls from the toolbox (item b) and dropping them on the form. If you choose to create a console application (i.e., an application without a GUI), the central area would display a Code window (e.g., Figure 1.4), where you could edit the J# code for your application.

Generally, J# application GUIs are made up of a series of one or more forms, onto which you have dragged and dropped components from the toolbox (buttons, textboxes, drop-down lists, etc.). In Figure 1.3, we have placed a single button on Form1, the only form in the project at this time.

If you double-click on any component in the Design window (including the form itself) Visual Studio will open the Code window for Form1 and place the cursor in an appropriate location; that is, if you double-click on the Button in Figure 1.3, Visual Studio will open to the code for that particular button object in Form1.jsl, as shown in Figure 1.4. All the code and design information for an individual form is stored inside a .jsl file.

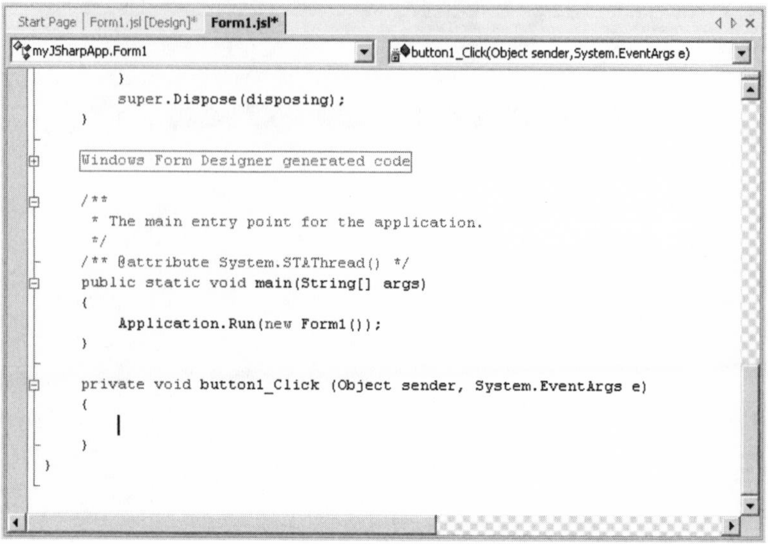

```
Start Page | Form1.jsl [Design]*  Form1.jsl*                                    ◁ ▷ ✕

❖ my JSharpApp.Form1                    ▼  ❖ button1_Click(Object sender,System.EventArgs e)  ▼

              )
         super.Dispose(disposing);
       )

⊞  ┌──────────────────────────────────┐
   │Windows Form Designer generated code│
   └──────────────────────────────────┘
⊟
       /**
        * The main entry point for the application.
        */
⊟      /** @attribute System.STAThread() */
       public static void main(String[] args)
       {
            Application.Run(new Form1());
       }

⊟      private void button1_Click (Object sender, System.EventArgs e)
       {
            |
       }
   )
```

Figure 1.4 Code view for **Form1** *in Figure 1.3 after a double-click*

Note that the method button1_Click() is actually a *handler* for the event triggered by clicking the button. That is, the button1_Click() method will activate (or *fire*) whenever the button is clicked. We'll look at events and handlers in more detail in Chapter 4.

The Toolbox (b)
The toolbox is a collection of all the controls you can place in your J# applications. It contains everything from simple controls like textboxes and labels to complex components like database adapters and status bars. The toolbox is divided into various categories that you can move among by clicking on their titles (Data, Components, Windows Forms, etc.). The default category for basic Windows applications is Windows Forms; most of the examples in this book will only use controls from that section of the toolbox.

The Solution Explorer (c)
The Solution Explorer allows you to view the layout of your entire solution. Microsoft refers to a collection of one or more projects, each of which can be in a different language and is stored in its own directory, as a *solution*. In the Solution Explorer pane, you can collapse and expand items to see what files currently reside in your project. As you can see in the upper right corner of Figure 1.3, Visual Studio generates a few nec-

essary files when you create a new project, all of which show up in the Solution Explorer.

As an alternative to the Solution Explorer, you can also get a class view of your project by clicking on the Class View tab. This will show your project as a hierarchy of classes, interfaces, and methods, as shown in Figure 1.5. Double-clicking a method of a class in this view will bring you to that method in the source code.

The Output Window (d)
The Output section of the IDE contains a variety of information, depending on what you're currently doing with your application. At the bottom of Figure 1.3, the Output section shows the compilation and debug messages from the most recent execution of this application. (When you first start a project, this region will be blank.) During execution, this area of the screen will be used to display build and debugging information (we'll talk more about building and debugging in the "Debugger" section later in this chapter).

The Properties Explorer (e)
The Properties Explorer is an area of the IDE with which you'll become very familiar by the time you finish this book. Each control on a form, including the Form object itself, has a set of adjustable properties that can

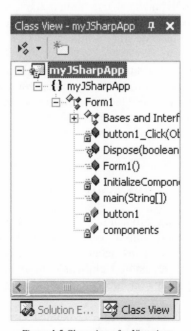

Figure 1.5 Class view of a J# project

be edited in the Properties Explorer. In Figure 1.3, for example, we have selected the "Hello" button in the Design window, and its properties are therefore showing in the Properties Explorer. As you can see, its Text property has been changed to read "Hello!" instead of the default (which will be something generic like "Button"). Common properties for controls include location, color, text content, size, and behavior. Most controls will have special properties specific to their functionality—a MonthCalendar control, for example, will have a TodayDate property.

There are a host of other components you can choose to display in your personalized IDE, most of which can be selected and configured from the View menu. You should see your Visual Studio .NET documentation for complete details.

THE DEBUGGER

Visual Studio .NET has a sophisticated debugging system, which, in the event of a bug, allows you to step through your applications one line of code at a time and monitor the values and behavior of all methods and variables. Debugging is accomplished mainly through the use of *breakpoints,* which are user-assigned points in a code listing at which you will be returned to the IDE and be able to observe the flow of the application from a code standpoint, rather than from the GUI. You can then execute the remainder of your code line by line in order to determine exactly where errors occur.

You can find instructions on how to use Visual Studio .NET's debugging tools (see Figure 1.6) to debug your console, Windows, and ASP.NET applications at ᴄᴺ⮑JS010002. Before trying to take advantage of the debugger, however, it may be helpful to read Chapters 3 and 4 of this book to learn how to design basic applications.

DYNAMIC HELP

Visual Studio .NET has a dynamic help system that is accessible from the main IDE screen. The tab to open Dynamic Help is located next to the Properties tab, which is by default in the bottom right corner of the screen. Basically, the Dynamic Help window provides contextual help, which changes depending on the object you have highlighted in the Design window.

For example, Figure 1.7 shows the Dynamic Help window display that appears when a Button object is highlighted in the Design window. As

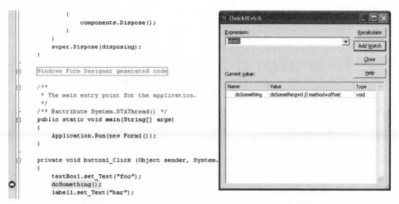

```
                (
                    components.Dispose();
                )
            )
            super.Dispose(disposing);
        )

    Windows Form Designer generated code

    /**
     * The main entry point for the application.
     */
    /** @attribute System.STAThread() */
    public static void main(String[] args)
    (
        Application.Run(new Form1());
    )

    private void button1_Click (Object sender, System.
    (
        textBox1.set_Text("foo");
        doSomething();
        label1.set_Text("bar");
```

QuickWatch

Expression:
label1

Recalculate
Add Watch
Close
Help

Current value:

Name	Value	Type
doSomething	doSomething+0 // method+offset	void

Watch 1

Name	Value	Type
□ label1	{System.Windows.Forms.Label}	System.W
⊞ System.Windows.Forn	{System.Windows.Forms.Label}	System.W
AutoSize	false	boolean
BackgroundImage	\<undefined value>	System.D
BorderStyle	None	System.W

Autos   Locals   Watch 1

Figure 1.6 Debugging tools in VS .NET

Figure 1.7 Dynamic Help for a button object

you can see, the window gives immediate access to help documentation on the Button class, members of that class, and other more general documentation on Windows Form design and Visual Studio. In the code view of an application, placing the cursor on certain keywords (such as namespace names) will also trigger a change in the Dynamic Help window.

Clicking on any of the links in the Dynamic Help window will open an HTML document containing the relevant information in the central panel of the screen.

Remember that all of the help files and documentation for Visual Studio .NET and its languages can also be found in the MSDN Library documentation online (msdn.microsoft.com) or installed on your machine (if you chose to do so).

What Is This Book?

This book is intended as an introduction to J# development in Visual Studio .NET for students or developers who are already familiar with, or are in the process of learning, the Java language. Throughout this book, we will look at various aspects of the J# programming language and how Microsoft extensions, GUI development tools, and Web features can be used to extend and improve your Java applications. By the time you finish reading *CodeNotes for J#,* you should be as comfortable working with J# as you are with Java, and you will be ready to start designing large-scale applications using all the basic features of the .NET Framework.

CHAPTER OUTLINE

CodeNotes for J# is divided into eight chapters that cover the following topics:

1. Introduction: The chapter you are currently reading introduces you to the core concepts behind the .NET Framework, Visual Studio .NET development, and J# itself. If you have never programmed using Microsoft development tools before or you are unfamiliar with integrated development environments in general, we recommend that you read this chapter from start to finish to get an idea of what programming in J# will be like.

2. Installation: In order to follow along with the code samples and topical examples in this book, you will need to have various technologies installed on your machine. This chapter provides instructions for obtaining and installing all the necessary applications.

3. Basic Java and the CLR: Although you should already be familiar with basic Java, this chapter provides a brief overview of Java syntax, commands, and commenting structures, as well as reviews of concepts such as exceptions, error handling, and inheritance, to see how they are handled in J#. It then moves on to a discussion on extending Java using the .NET Framework and discusses some of the parallels between the Framework and Java core libraries.

4. Windows Forms: We will introduce concepts of GUI development using Windows Forms and show how you can create complex user interfaces by simply dragging and dropping components from a toolbox. In this section, we will also discuss events, delegates, and event handlers, and show how Windows components use these to make your user interface (UI) work the way you want it to. Finally, we will briefly examine GDI+, a powerful graphics-rendering library.

5. ASP.NET: With .NET, Microsoft has begun to shift its core development focus to the Web. ASP.NET, the latest generation of Microsoft's Active Server Pages, is a set of technologies for developing and deploying dynamic Web Applications. In this chapter, we provide an overview of how to create Web Applications in J# and ASP.NET, and we discuss how ASP.NET Web Forms can be used to provide similar functionality to Windows Forms in an online environment.

6. Web Services: Web Services are applications that allow any number of machines to communicate information to one another via HTTP and XML messages. Web Services are becoming extremely important to many modern online businesses, and this book will show you the basics of the various XML technologies involved and how to leverage them in creating your own Web Service applications.

7. Marine Biology Case Study in .NET: The Java edition of the Advanced Placement (AP) Computer Science Program uses a large case study to familiarize students with good coding, design, documentation, and testing practices, and to give them experience with development on a larger scale than they would normally get in the classroom. In this chapter, we will introduce

the case study and look at how various .NET technologies such as ASP.NET and Web Services can be used to extend the case study in interesting ways.
8. Advanced topics: Finally, we will look at some important .NET technologies that are not part of the required AP curriculum but play a vital role in most real-world development practices. This chapter will provide brief overviews and examples of ADO.NET (database access), remoting (allowing applications in two different CLRs to work together), and other technologies beyond the scope of an introductory book.

MARINE BIOLOGY CASE STUDY

This book was originally developed as a supplementary text for the AP computer science courses that are taught at many schools throughout the United States. These courses are intended for high school level students who are advanced in the area of computer science and therefore require courses that are more challenging to their current skill sets. The Marine Biology Case Study, discussed in Chapter 7 of this book, is intended to be used as a teaching tool in AP computer science classes. However, because nonstudent readers will also find looking at a case study extremely helpful, links to complete details and downloadable code for the application can be found at ⌐CN⌐ JS010003.

Although a C++ version of the Marine Biology Case Study already exists, the Java version will be introduced in the 2003–2004 school year. According to the College Board website's description (www. collegeboard.com/ap/students/compsci/download.html), using a case study in a classroom setting allows students to do the following:

• Read source code written by someone else.
• Work with a program of significant length.
• Become familiar with good coding, design, and documentation practice.
• Learn about testing in a nontrivial context.
• Think through design and implementation trade-offs.
• Experience an approximation of the master/apprentice relationship.

The Marine Biology Case Study, in particular, is an account of the summer job experiences of Pat, a computer science student. Pat is assigned to make changes to an existing application that models fish moving in a body of water. Students will read about how Pat learns the inner workings of the original simulator program. They will follow along as she plans and adds modifications to the system according to instructions from the resident biologists, and then tests her addition using tried-and-true methods.

The introduction to the case study explains as follows:

A simulation is a model of a real system. Scientists build simulations to better understand the systems they are studying, to observe and predict their behavior, or to perform experiments on them. Many real systems are difficult or impossible to observe and control, much less experiment with. It is easy, though, to run a simulation program repeatedly and to modify it to explore the effect of changes to the model.

I worked on a simulation of fish moving in a relatively small body of water, such as a lake. The modifications I added made the simulation more interesting and allowed the biologists to study more complex behavior. For example, one change I made allowed the biologists to track the fish population as fish breed and die. Another change allowed them to study what happens when there are several kinds of fish in the environment, with different patterns of movement.

Figure 1.8 shows a screen capture from the original version of the simulation, before Pat has had a chance to make any changes.

Chapter 7 of this CodeNotes will discuss some ways that the Marine Biology Simulator demonstrated in the AP course can be extended using .NET technologies. In particular, we will add a new kind of fish to the environment using Visual Studio .NET IDE and then design a Web Service that will allow users to download remote MBS environments for use in their own applications.

You can find links to more information on the AP computer science program and the Marine Biology Case Study at ⌐ᴄ̃ᴺ JS010003.

Chapter Summary

This introductory chapter provides the basic background information you need to understand the material presented in the rest of this book. By now you should understand the basics of the Visual Studio .NET Integrated Development Environment, such as how to start new solutions and projects and how to get relevant help documentation when you need it.

This chapter also discusses the .NET Framework itself, and how applications written in any .NET language (J#, C#, VB.NET, etc.) are compiled to assemblies containing intermediate language (MSIL). Assemblies can then be executed on any machine with a Common Language Runtime (CLR). The CLR is conceptually similar to a Java

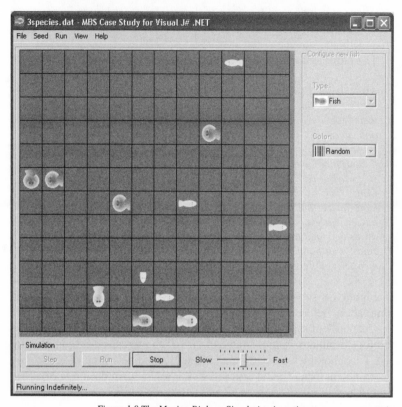

Figure 1.8 The Marine Biology Simulation in action

Virtual Machine (JVM), in that it allows cross-platform compatibility of applications written on a specific platform. The remainder of the *Code-Notes for J#* will delve deeper into the specific features of VS .NET, the Base Class Library, the J# language, and the capabilities J# will give you thanks to the .NET Framework.

Chapter 2

—

INSTALLATION

This chapter contains installation instructions for all of the technologies used in this book. After completing these directions, you will be able to compile and run the sample code found in each chapter. Most of the software used in this book is straightforward to install, and we recommend that you use the default settings whenever possible.

The three main components needed to complete the samples in this book include the .NET Framework redistributable, the J# redistributable, and the J# compiler. The .NET Framework redistributable includes the runtime and class libraries required to run *any* .NET application. The J# redistributable adds the class libraries required to run J# applications. And the J# compiler builds .NET assemblies (DLLs and EXEs) from your Java-language source code.

The first two components (the .NET Framework redistributable and the J# redistributable) are available as free downloads from Microsoft's website. The third component (J# compiler) can also be downloaded for free along with the .NET Framework SDK (which also includes compilers for C#, VB.NET, and C++). The .NET Framework SDK is great for developers who want to use their own text editor (Notepad, Emacs, etc.). Developers who prefer a richer and more productive development environment will want to take advantage of Visual Studio .NET, which now includes the J# compiler. For instructions on finding these components, see ⚭ JS020001. (This pointer will also detail some options for getting low-cost evaluation versions of Visual Studio .NET.)

Throughout this chapter you will encounter hyperlinks to installation components or additional software. At the time of writing, all links are correct. However, please see ⟨CN⟩JS020003 for any updated link information on the components found in this chapter or throughout the book.

.NET System Requirements

The .NET Framework can be installed on most Windows operating systems, including Windows 2000, Windows 98, Windows ME, Windows NT, Windows Server 2003, and Windows XP. However, the system requirements are dependent on the actual OS version. In addition, ASP.NET applications require IIS 5.0 or later. IIS 5.0 cannot be installed on Windows ME or Windows 98. Finally, if you intend to use Visual Studio .NET, your system requirements will increase. Consult the product documentation or Microsoft's websites for the latest information.

.NET Distribution

The following instructions are for installing Visual Studio .NET 2003. If you have an earlier version of VS .NET, the process may be slightly different. VS .NET 2003 is the recommended environment for developing with J#, so we encourage you to upgrade if you are using an earlier version. However, we include instructions for adding J# to earlier VS .NET versions later in this chapter.

For instructions on obtaining a copy of the .NET Framework and VS .NET, please see ⟨CN⟩JS020001. Once you have a version of the installation program, the instructions below will help you through the installation process.

Installing Visual Studio .NET and the .NET Framework

Whether you install from multiple CDs, a single DVD, or one large file, the basic process is the same. For the purposes of this book, we will assume you are working with the four-CD set. However, if you are using a different install, the only change will be that all of the files will be in one place rather than split onto multiple disks.

To install the .NET Framework and Visual Studio .NET, run SETUP.EXE, found on the first CD or from the download. After a couple of minutes you will be greeted with the screen shown in Figure 2.1. As Figure 2.1 indicates, you must install the Visual Studio .NET Prerequisites before installing VS .NET. The prerequisites include the .NET Framework and any critical system updates required for .NET to work. For more details on what actually gets installed in this step, see ⊶JS020004. Depending on your system, you may already have all of the prerequisites installed, in which case you can skip to step 2.

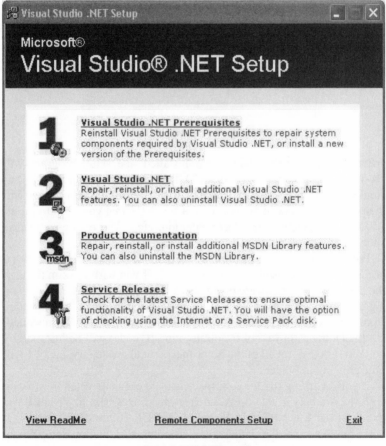

Figure 2.1 VS .NET setup

INSTALLING PREREQUISITES

After clicking Visual Studio .NET Prerequisites, the setup program will analyze your machine for a few minutes to determine which system files need to be updated. Depending on the operating system and the applications that you have already installed, the setup program may have to reboot the system several times during the installation process. Because of this requirement, it offers the Automatic Log On feature; by entering your password into the installation program, the system can automatically log on and continue the installation every time it has to reboot the machine. The setup program may have to reboot the machine as many as seven times during the installation routine, which means this option can be a real time-saver. If you disable this option, you will have to log on to the machine each time the computer reboots.

After you either enable or disable Automatic Log On (a simple checkbox), the setup program will begin installing the prerequisites. Depending on the files it must update, this procedure could take several minutes. During this time, the setup program will detail its progress, as illustrated in Figure 2.2.

INSTALLING VISUAL STUDIO .NET

After the prerequisites have been installed, the setup program will prompt you for the first VS .NET CD. If you installed from the DVD or single file, the location will be automatically selected. The installer will then ask you to choose the portions of VS .NET that you want to install (the individual languages documentation, etc.). The options screen is shown in Figure 2.3.

For working with the examples in this book, we recommend that you accept the default install options. However, if you wish to skim through the list of options, be aware that a check mark indicates installation, and a grayed-out box indicates that only some components will be installed from that section. In other words, Visual C++ will be partially installed, but the Dotfuscator (a tool for obfuscating IL code) will be installed by default. If you select all of the items in a particular category, the box will go from gray to white.

If you are trying to save disk space and are only interested in working with the samples in this book, uncheck the boxes next to Visual Basic .NET, Visual C# .NET, and Visual C++ .NET. If you decide later that you want to add another language, it's as simple as running Setup again.

After selecting the aspects of VS .NET that you want included (J# is found under Language Tools in Figure 2.3), click **Install Now.** The

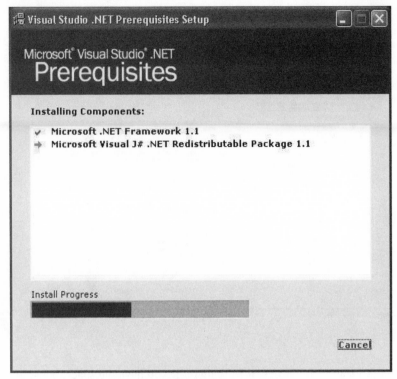

Figure 2.2 Installing .NET prerequisites

setup program will begin. Depending on the options that you have selected, installation could take anywhere from 20 to 60 minutes. After the
installation has finished, your computer will contain all the necessary
tools to build and deploy .NET applications.

PRODUCT DOCUMENTATION AND SERVICE RELEASES

Step 3 (Product Documentation) and Step 4 (System Updates), of the VS
.NET Setup screen in Figure 2.1 are optional. Step 3, Product Documentation, will install the Microsoft Developer Network (MSDN) Library documentation on your machine. The documentation is a
complete, comprehensive resource on every class, method, and feature
of the Base Class Library (BCL) and the operation of Visual Studio
.NET. However, it will take up approximately 2 GB of additional storage
on your hard drive, so if space is an issue, you may want to use the
MSDN Library from the CDs (if you have them), or install it on a net-

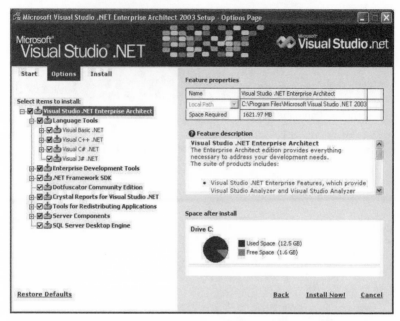

Figure 2.3 VS .NET installation screen

work location and access it from there. If you have the space, however, it is recommended that you install MSDN Library locally.

Step 4, System Updates, allows you to check for the latest service releases of the .NET Framework and Visual Studio .NET. At the time of this writing there are no service releases for VS .NET 2003. However, clicking this option will search the Internet for any available updates and give you the option of installing them if they are found. It is a good idea to click this option before completing the installation, just to make sure you aren't missing anything important. You can always invoke this option again from Visual Studio .NET by selecting **Help → Check for Updates.**

PROGRAM LOCATIONS

The Visual Studio .NET 2003 setup program will append two new items to your Start menu's Program folder. The first item is called Microsoft .NET Framework SDK 1.1, and it contains SDK documentation and code samples. The second item is called Microsoft Visual Studio .NET 2003, and it contains links to the VS .NET IDE and to another folder called Visual Studio .NET Tools. In this book we will frequently build programs from the VS .NET command line, which you can access by clicking the Visual Studio .NET 2003 Command Prompt icon shown in Figure 2.4. This prompt simply adds the `\%ProgramFiles%\Microsoft Visual Studio .NET\FrameworkSDK\Bin` directory to your PATH so that you can access and run the .NET Framework command-line utilities from within any directory.

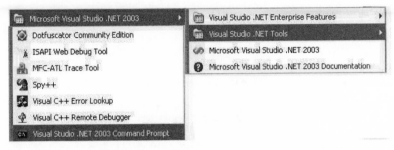

Figure 2.4 The Visual Studio .NET Command Prompt

Installing J#

If you followed the instructions in the previous section, you will now have an up-to-date version of the .NET Framework and Visual Studio .NET on your computer, including all of the required J# elements. However, note that older versions of the Visual Studio 2002 .NET setup did not automatically include support for J#. If you have previously used an older version of the VS .NET install (you would know because J# would not be present in your New Project menu), this section will demonstrate how J# may be installed.

Visual J# .NET can be obtained in the form of a small (18-MB), self-extracting archive from Microsoft's MSDN website. At the time of this writing, the English-language version of this file is called `VJSharpSetup.exe`. It is available free from http://msdn.microsoft.com/vjsharp/, although you can also check ⚓JS020003 for updated links.

After obtaining this file, double-click on it. You will see the window shown in Figure 2.5.

Visual J# .NET requires that you first install a redistributable package, which contains all of the core classes necessary for building J# code. Simply click the "1" button, as shown in Figure 2.5, and follow the instructions in the ordinary Windows installer. When the redistributable package is installed, the "2" button will become available. You will then

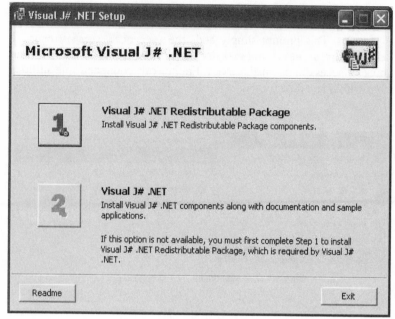

Figure 2.5 Installing Visual J# .NET

be able to complete the installation of Visual J# .NET by installing the VS .NET editor component. Once again, simply follow the instructions in the installer.

Remember, however, that you do not need to install J# as a separate piece unless you are using a pre-2003 version of Visual Studio .NET that does not already have support for J# applications.

Other J# Tools

Although you will usually work with J# from the VS .NET environment, you should also be aware of several command-line tools that may help you with Java programs. These tools are briefly introduced here and are illustrated throughout the book.

- **jbimp.exe** This is the Microsoft Java language bytecode–to–MSIL converter. This program can be used to convert compiled Java code (`.class` files) into Microsoft IL code, which can be executed on the .NET platform. You may need to use this tool if you wish to convert existing code for which you no longer have the source files. For more on JBIMP, see ⌐CN⌐JS020005.

- **vjc.exe** This is the command-line compiler for J#. This program is similar in functionality to the javac.exe program installed with the Java Developer's Kit. VJC compiles your Java-language source code into .NET assemblies that can be executed by the Common Language Runtime. We used this tool in Chapter 1 and will cover it again in the beginning of Chapter 3.
- **ILDASM.exe** This is a decompiler for .NET assemblies. If you want to look into a .NET assembly and examine the instructions and metadata that make up the assembly, this is the tool to use. It's roughly equivalent to using javaw.exe to examine a JAR file; however, ILDASM goes one step further and actually allows you to explore the IL code inside each class in the assembly. You may realize from Chapter 1 that ILDASM is not specific to J#, as all .NET languages compile to IL.

Marine Biology Simulation Case Study

In Chapter 7 of this book, we will examine the AP Marine Biology Case Study and how it can be expanded upon using the technologies included in .NET (such as Windows Forms, ASP.NET, and Web Services). In order to follow along with the examples in Chapter 7, you will need to install the case study source code on your machine. Please see JS020006 for instructions on how to download and install the Microsoft version of the Marine Biology Case Study.

Installing Internet Information Services (IIS)
If you want to work with ASP.NET or Web Services, you will need to install Microsoft Internet Information Services (IIS) version 5.0 or later. Depending on your operating system, IIS may already be installed. For complete instructions on how to install IIS and verify that it is working with .NET, see JS050001.

Chapter 3

—

BASIC J#

J# is the first initiative to allow Java language developers to program in their native language and still take advantage of *all* of the features of the .NET Framework, including Windows-based applications (Windows Forms, Chapter 4 of this CodeNotes), Web-based applications (ASP.NET Web Forms, Chapter 5), and XML Web Services (Chapter 6).

Most Java applications written using the core Java libraries (JDK 1.1.4) can be compiled as J# and incorporated into a Visual Studio .NET solution. J# applications will not necessarily compile using the Java compiler (javac.exe), however, because Microsoft has taken the Java programming language and given J# developers the ability to access the full gamut of libraries that ship with the .NET Framework. This means that J# is more than just the Java language—J# is the Java language *plus* the class libraries *plus* all the tools included in Visual Studio .NET (such as the Windows Form Designer). If you don't want to use the VS .NET IDE you can still write J# in a text editor and compile from the command prompt, just as you might with ordinary Java.

In this chapter, we will begin by reviewing the basics of J# syntax. Remember that if you are familiar with the Java language then you already know J#, since the syntax is identical. We will also look at the syntax for error handling and object-oriented concepts such as inheritance. In the second topic, we will examine how J# applications can be extended beyond JDK functionality using the libraries in the .NET Framework, a set of thousands of classes and interfaces that are accessible by every .NET language. We will examine the differences between the

.NET Framework Libraries and the JDK libraries, see how J# has been adapted to use .NET data types instead of Java, and compare .NET solutions to Java packages and Java Archive (JAR) files for application deployment.

Simple Application

Before jumping into detailed aspects of J#, let's look at a very simple example. The following simple application demonstrates how basic Java skills will allow you to create applications that compile as either Java or J# programs.

Working with Text Editors

We're going to create a J# application in the simplest manner possible. Since we don't need the full power of VS .NET, start by opening your favorite text editor. If you don't have a favorite editor, notepad.exe will work well. Type the code in Listing 3.1.

```
public class TempConvert
{
  public static void main(String[] args)
  {
    double tempInC = Double.parseDouble(args[0]);
    double tempInF = 1.8 * tempInC + 32;
    System.out.println(tempInC + " degrees Celsius equals " +
                       tempInF + " degrees Fahrenheit.");
  }
}
```

Listing 3.1 Simple temperature conversion application

Save this file as TempConvert.java. Note that the main() method in TempConvert accepts a single parameter from the command line representing a temperature in Celsius, converts it to a temperature in Fahrenheit, and then prints the results to the console. Because this is meant to be an extremely simple example, we are not performing any error checking.

Now that we have written our program and saved it to disk, open a Visual Studio .NET Command Prompt (**Visual Studio .NET 2003 → Visual Studio .NET Tools → Visual Studio .NET Command Prompt**). Remember that the Visual Studio .NET Command Prompt is just like an ordinary command prompt, except that all the .NET command-line utilities (compilers, conversion tools, etc.) will be available from any directory. As we saw in Chapter 1, a .java file can be compiled and run using either traditional Java utilities (javac.exe and java.exe) or using Microsoft's command-line J# compiler (vjc.exe). Listing 3.2 and Listing 3.3, respectively, demonstrate these approaches, with the command-line commands in bold. If you have the Java Developers Kit (JDK) properly installed, you can compile with javac.exe and run your program with java.exe, as shown in Listing 3.2.

```
C:\>javac TempConvert.java
C:\>java TempConvert 32
32.0 degrees Celsius equals 89.6 degrees Fahrenheit.
```

Listing 3.2 Compiling and running TempConvert *in traditional Java*

If, however, you want to compile with J#, you will want to use the vjc.exe compiler, as shown in Listing 3.3.

```
C:\>vjc TempConvert.java
Microsoft (R) Visual J# .NET Compiler version 7.10.2292.0
for Microsoft (R) .NET Framework version 1.1.4322
Copyright (C) Microsoft Corp 2000-2002. All rights reserved.

C:\>TempConvert 32
32.0 degrees Celsius equals 89.6 degrees Fahrenheit.
```

Listing 3.3 Compiling and running TempConvert *using the J# compiler*

One significant difference you'll notice is that there's no need to use a tool like java.exe to run J# applications. Once a J# application is compiled, it is a self-supporting executable application that can be run completely independent of any helper programs (although it still requires the .NET Framework).

Working with the VS .NET IDE

One of the primary advantages of J# is that it is supported by the Visual Studio .NET IDE. Let's incorporate the TempConvert application into a full-fledged VS .NET solution.

Open Visual Studio .NET, click the **New Project** button, and select a new J# console application from the Templates list. A *console application* is an application that does not involve a GUI and runs from a command prompt. You will have to scroll down in the Templates list to see this template. Name your application TempConvert, and choose the default directory for your project.

Visual Studio .NET will then create a complete solution for you, as shown in Figure 3.1. The solution includes the following files:

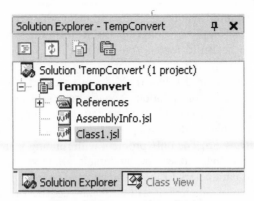

Figure 3.1 A new console application

- `TempConvert.sln` A data file that is used by VS .NET to represent the solution. It contains basic information about the solution, such as its name and the projects it contains. Note that the `.sln` file does not appear as a file in Solution Explorer since you will never need to edit it manually.
- `TempConvert.vsproj` A file with information on the project you just created (we have only one in the solution at the moment, but we can have multiple projects in one solution if we like). Like the `.sln` file, the `.vsproj` file does not appear as a file in Solution Explorer. Instead, each project file is represented by a project name (e.g., "TempConvert" in Figure 3.1).
- `AssemblyInfo.jsl` This file contains a set of attributes that provide information to the compiler about how an application should be compiled into an assembly. Although attributes are beyond the scope of this CodeNotes, you will see some examples in Chapter 6 when we discuss Web Services.
- `Class1.jsl` This is a starting-point file that contains a simple class declaration and an empty `main()` method that you can fill in.

We've already written our class file, so we don't need `Class1.jsl` in our project; right-click on it in the Solution Explorer and select. Now we need to add `TempConvert.java` to the project. Right-click on the `TempConvert` project (the project name, not "Solution 'TempConvert' ") in the Solution Explorer and select **Add Existing Item.** Browse to the location where you saved `TempConvert.java` and click on the file name to select it. Click **OK** to add `TempConvert.java` to the project. Notice how both `.jsl` and `.java` files are allowed in J# projects. The J# compiler will handle files with either extension.

You can now take advantage of all the tools available in Visual Studio, such as dynamic syntax checking and debugging. You can compile your application simply by selecting **Build Solution** or **Build Temp-Convert** from the **Build** menu. You will find the compiled assembly, TempConvert.exe, in the My Documents \Visual Studio Projects \TempConvert\bin\debug folder (unless you specified a different location when you created the solution). You can run TempConvert.exe from the command line as you did in the first part of this simple application.

It is also possible to run your application directly from VS .NET by pressing **CTRL + F5.** The only problem with running your application from VS .NET is that it does not, by default, allow you to specify any command-line parameters to the application. If you try running Temp-Convert with no parameters, it will throw an IndexOutOfBounds exception, indicating that main() is looking for a value that doesn't exist. To supply command-line parameters using VS .NET, right-click on the TempConvert project and select **Properties.** This will open a new window called Property Pages. You will see two folders—Common Properties and Configuration Properties—in a list box on the left. Click on **Configuration Properties,** and scroll down in the list of properties until you find the **Start Options** group. Add a numerical value to the **Command Line Arguments** property, as shown in Figure 3.2.

Note that running an application from VS .NET by pressing **CTRL + F5** executes the application without debugging. One advantage to using

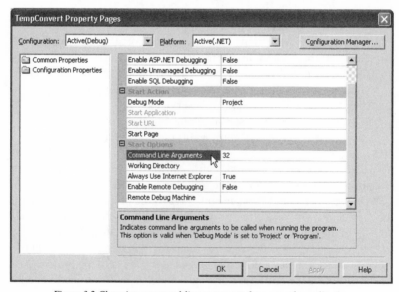

Figure 3.2 Changing command-line arguments for a console application

CTRL + F5 instead of simply F5 for console applications is that it provides the friendly "Press any key to continue" message when the program is finished running, so you can see the program's final output before returning to the IDE.

CORE CONCEPTS

J# Command-Line Compiler (VJC.EXE)

In the first part of Listing 3.2, we compiled our simple application (TempConvert) using vjc.exe with no additional compiler options. When compiling J# programs from the command line, you will usually not need any compiler options. For other examples in this chapter, you will be able to use the compiler exactly as you did in the simple application—with no compiler options. However, there are several options you might find useful in certain circumstances. In general, vjc.exe compiler options are used as shown in Listing 3.4.

```
vjc /option:value sourcefile.java
```

Listing 3.4 Using vjc.exe *with options*

The following are some useful compiler options:

- **/out**   Allows you to specify a file name other than the default to which your application will be compiled. For example, vjc /out:MyProg.exe sourcefile.java would create MyProg.exe instead of sourcefile.exe.
- **/target**   Allows you to specify the kind of application or assembly you are creating. Possible values are for console applications (exe), Windows Forms applications (winexe), complete code libraries (library), and modules (module). (Modules are essentially small libraries that aren't as fully formed, which are often used for internationalization.) For example, vjc /target:library sourcefile.java would create sourcefile.dll.
- **/recurse**   Allows you to specify a wildcard string and compile all files in the current directory *and* any subdirectories that match that wildcard. For example, vjc /recurse *.java would compile all .java files in the current directory and in any subdirectories underneath it.

There are many other compiler options that range from the obscure to the very advanced. You can see a list of them with brief descriptions by simply typing vjc (with no options or file names) at a command line. You can find more information on using the vjc.exe compiler options at ᴄᴺ⟩JS030001.

STRUCTURE OF A CLASS FILE

The structure of a J# class is identical to that of a Java class. The following rules will help you structure your classes correctly.

- A basic class declaration looks like Listing 3.5. All variable and method declarations go inside the curly braces { }.

```
public class MyClass
{ }
```

Listing 3.5 A class declaration in J#

- In Java, a public class must be in a file with the same name as the class. For example, the class MyClass in Listing 3.5 must be written in a file named MyClass.java. when using the Java compiler; otherwise, javac.exe will report an error. This is *not* the case in J#: you can name your file anything you want and the application will still compile properly. In addition, you can also have multiple public classes in a single file—this is a significant difference from traditional Java.
- In both Java and J# applications, each application must have a starting point. This means that at least one public class must have the method shown in Listing 3.6.

```
public static void main(String[] args)
```

Listing 3.6 The main method

This is the main driver method for the application and is what the execution engine will look for when you try to run the application. Note that when you add a new class to a J# solution using Visual Studio .NET, it will not add the main() method for you. If you don't have a main() somewhere else, you'll have to add it or your application will not run.

- In addition to main(), classes can contain as many other methods as you like. Basic method declaration takes the form in Listing 3.7.

```
[public/private] [return type] [method name] (arguments)
```

Listing 3.7 A generic method prototype

For example, we might declare a method as in Listing 3.8.

```
public boolean isOdd(int i)
```

Listing 3.8 A simple method

We'll discuss the public, private, and other modifiers further in the "Visibility" section later in this chapter.

- Any J# class can have one or more *constructor* methods that will execute when an instance of the class is created. Typically, constructors contain initialization code for the class. A constructor is declared as a method with the same name as the class it is in and without a return value. Several constructors for `myClass` are shown in Listing 3.9.

```
public class myClass
{
  private String name;

  public myClass()
  {
    this.name = "Guest";
  }
  public myClass(String n)
  {
    this.name = n;
  }
}
```

Listing 3.9 Constructors

Topic: J# Core Syntax

In this topic, we will provide a brief review of basic J# syntax, error handling, and inheritance. If you are already quite comfortable with basic Java language syntax, you might want to skip the rest of this chapter and go straight to Chapter 4 ("Windows Forms"). If you're new to the Java language as well as to J#, we recommend that you take the time to read this chapter, which will help you brush up on the essentials before continuing with the rest of this book. From Chapter 4 on, we will assume you are already familiar with concepts such as statements, looping, and decision making.

In general, you should already be somewhat familiar with most of the material in this topic. If you have never programmed using the Java language before, please see ⌐ᶜᴺᵧJS030002 for some links to additional tutorials and background materials before continuing.

CONCEPTS

Basic Syntax
In the following sections, we'll quickly review the most important syntactical features that are used throughout this CodeNotes.

Comments
J# comments are exactly the same as Java comments. Single-line comments are prefixed by //. Multiline comments should be surrounded by /* and */ sequences. Listing 3.10 shows an example.

```
// this is a single-line comment
/* This comment is really long, and therefore we have to use
multiline comment style in order to fit everything in. */
```

Listing 3.10 Using comments in J#

Note that J# also supports JavaDoc comment syntax for creating HTML documentation from your code. You can initiate a JavaDoc block by typing /**; J# will add the closing sequence for you and will allow you to enter various parameters by beginning comment lines with an @ symbol. Visual Studio .NET also includes the ability to generate HTML documentation for your application from the JavaDoc comments in your code. For more information on using JavaDoc in J#, see ⌐ᶜᴺᵧJS030003.

Variables
A variable in J# is a named data type or object. For example, we can declare an integer variable named myInt with the line of code shown in Listing 3.11.

```
// declare an integer variable with a null value
int myInt;
```

Listing 3.11 Declaring an integer

We can also initialize variables (that is, give them a value) at the same time we declare them. Listing 3.12 creates a new String variable and initializes it with a value of "foo".

```
// declare a String variable and initialize it
// with a value of "foo"
String myString = "foo";
```

Listing 3.12 Declaring a variable

Remember that variables have *scope*, meaning that they are valid only inside the block of code in which they are declared, as well as in any nested blocks of code. For a brief review of variable scope rules, please see ◦ᴺᐟJS030004.

Arrays

.NET arrays are 0-based, just like Java arrays, so declaration of array variables has not changed. You can declare both one-dimensional and multidimensional arrays, and initialize array variables upon creation, as shown in Listing 3.13.

```
//empty integer array
int foo[];

//Array of twenty String elements
String bar[] = new String[20];

//Multidimensional array
boolean multi[] [];

//Initialized five element array
int combination[5] = {3, 8, 29, 20, 15};
```

Listing 3.13 Declaring arrays

Looping

J# supports three different control flow statements, which allow you to repeat a block of code. The block of code can be set to loop a specified number of times or until a certain condition is met.

- A for statement allows you to repeat a block of code a certain number of times. Basically, you do the following:
    1. Initialize a "counter" variable to a certain value.
    2. Provide a condition or a limit for the counter, after which the block of code should no longer run.
    3. Specify an increment by which the counter should increase (or decrease) toward that limit.

For example, the `for` statement in Listing 3.14 creates a new variable named `i` and initializes it with a value of 0—this is our counter. We then specify that the loop should stop when the counter reaches 5, and that the counter should increment itself by 1 every time through the loop.

```
for (int i = 0; i < 5; i++)
{
  // this code will be run 5 times
}
```

Listing 3.14 A `for` *loop*

Note that `i++` is a shortcut that means the same thing as `i = i + 1`.

• A `while` statement is like a `for` statement except that, instead of incrementing a counter toward a certain limit, you simply set a condition after which the `while` loop will terminate. In Listing 3.15, for example, the loop will stop running when the `foo` variable has a value of 0. Any changes to your variable must happen inside the loop rather than in the loop declaration.

```
int foo = 7;

while (foo != 0)
{
  // this code will run until foo=0
  foo--;
}
```

Listing 3.15 A `while` *loop*

In most cases, `while` statements are better than `for` loops when you are not certain how many iterations it will take for a condition to become true.

• An alternative to a `while` statement is a `do-while` statement, which does exactly the same thing as a `while` statement except that it always runs the code in the block at least once. So, whereas the code in Listing 3.15 would never execute if `foo` equaled 0 when it arrived at the `while` loop, the code in the `do-while` statement in Listing 3.16 will execute at least once, no matter what the value of `foo` is.

```
do
{
```

```
// this code will run at least once, even if foo=0
} while (foo != 0)
```

Listing 3.16 A do-while loop

Note that you can break out of any of these looping blocks by inserting a break statement. This statement will end execution of the loop and proceed to the next statement after the loop.

Decision Making

Decision-making statements, also known as *conditional statements,* allow you to dictate that a certain block of code will execute only if a particular condition is met. Unlike looping statements, however, code inside a decision-making statement executes only once.

For shorter true-or-false conditions, the best thing to use is an if/else statement. Listing 3.17 shows an example of an if/else statement in which we "do something" if the integer variable count is greater than or equal to 5, and "do something else" if count is less than 5.

```
if (count >= 5)
{
  // do something
}
else
{
  // do something else
}
```

Listing 3.17 An if/else statement

We have created a binary branch in our program. In either branch, we perform an action. However, we can also create a scenario where we perform an action on only one branch by omitting the "else" condition. That is, if we modify Listing 3.17 and remove the "else" condition, we will take action only if count is greater than or equal to 5.

In some cases, you won't have a simple true/false condition. Rather, you will want to create a multipart check where a variable might have several possible values, each of which requires a distinct action. You can extend the if/else block to handle this case using the else if condition, as shown in Listing 3.18.

```
if (count >= 5)
{
  // do something
}
```

```
else if (count > 0)
{
  // do something else
}
else
{
  // if neither of the above apply, do this
}
```

Listing 3.18 Using else if

Long chains of if/else statements can be extremely cumbersome in an application, in terms of both the appearance of the code and the unanticipated logic bugs. If you want a larger, multifaceted decision structure, it is advisable to use a switch statement. A J# switch statement looks like Listing 3.19.

```
int i = -40;

switch (i)
{
  case 32:
    System.out.println("exciting!");
    break;
  case -40;
    System.out.println("party!");
    break;
  default:
    System.out.println("boring...");
};
```

Listing 3.19 A switch statement

The condition of a switch statement must be an ordinal value, meaning that it must be a variable of a type that can be ordered in some way. Ordinal types include int, char, String, and boolean (0 or 1). For each value of the condition you want to handle (values of i in Listing 3.19), you create a case. Case blocks actually execute sequentially, which means that if you don't put a break statement at the end of one case, the next case after it will also execute. This waterfall behavior will continue down the list of case blocks until another break statement or the end of the case structure is reached. The default statement is like an else statement, in that it will handle any cases that are not explicitly referred to elsewhere in the switch.

Printing

J# uses streams for input and output of text and data. A *stream* is simply data that is moving sequentially from one location to another. System.out is a special, predefined output stream that is typically used to send text strings from an application to the console (although it can be configured to output elsewhere as well). Specifically, if you want to print something to the console while your application is running, you would use one of two methods:

- System.out.print() takes a string as a parameter and outputs it to the console, without a line break at the end.
- System.out.println() takes a string as a parameter and outputs it to the console, with a line break at the end.

Both of these methods allow you to concatenate literal strings (e.g., "hi there") and string variables (e.g., String myString) on the fly using the + operator. Listing 3.20 shows several examples of the print() and println() methods.

```
String myName = "Craig";
// print a literal string with no line break
System.out.print("Hello there!");

// concatenate and print 2 literal strings with a line break
System.out.println("Hello" + " there!");

// concatenate literals and the name variable together
System.out.println("Hello " + myName + ", how are you?");
```

Listing 3.20 Using print() *and* println()

The output from these three lines would look like Listing 3.21.

```
Hello there!Hello there!
Hello Craig, how are you?
```

Listing 3.21 Output from Listing 3.20

Note that both of these methods are also overloaded to allow printing of other primitive data types such as int, double, float, and boolean. That is, the compiler will automatically convert the primitive data type into a valid string format before adding it to the current string or printing out the result. In addition, all of the built-in classes (such as the dateTime class) have a toString() method that allows them to be printed as strings using print() or println().

Return Statement

Every function must return a value equivalent to the data type in its declaration. For example, the function in Listing 3.22 must return an integer value.

```
public int randomInt() {}
```

Listing 3.22 A function declaration

In order to meet this rule, you can use the return statement, as shown in Listing 3.23. The return statement exits your function and returns control to the calling function.

```
class Foo
{
public static void main(String[] args)
{
  int i = 6;
  Foo myFoo = new foo();

  if (myFoo.isEven(i))
    System.out.println("It's even!");
  else
    System.out.println("It's odd!");
  }

  private boolean isEven(int myInt)
  {
    return ((myInt%2)==0);
  }
}
```

Listing 3.23 Using the return *statement*

The isEven() method shown in Listing 3.23 returns a boolean value—true if the supplied parameter is an even number and false in any other case. Note that because the equality operator (==) returns a boolean value, we don't need to use a decision structure (if/else) to determine our return value.

Remember that the value you return must honor your function declaration (e.g., isEven must return a boolean). However, if your function is declared as void, as is the main function in Listing 3.23, you have two choices:

- Omit the return keyword. If you omit the keyword, your function ends when the last line of code is executed. Most main() functions will end in this fashion.
- Use the return keyword without a value. If you use return without a value, you are effectively using the return keyword as a way to break out of your function. In most normal circumstances you will want to avoid this approach, as it creates multiple exit points from a function and can be confusing to another developer who is trying to interpret your function's logic.

In any case, the compiler will prevent you from misusing the return statement. If you declare a function as anything other than void, you will have to return an appropriate value.

ArrayList
An ArrayList is like a resizable array. It is actually an arraylike implementation of the List interface (we'll see more about interfaces in the "Inheritance" section later in this chapter). Basically, an ArrayList allows you to add (and remove) an unlimited number of elements, which can be of any nonprimitive type. Listing 3.24 shows an example of the various functions supported by an ArrayList object.

```
import java.util.*;

class Foo
{
  public static void main(String[] args)
  {
    ArrayList myAL = new ArrayList();

    // add some strings to the arraylist
    myAL.add("Larry");
    myAL.add("Curly");
    myAL.add("Moe");
    myAL.add("Shemp");

    // print out the entire ArrayList if it's not empty
    if (!myAL.isEmpty())
      System.out.println(myAL);

    // print out the second member of the ArrayList
    System.out.println(myAL.get(1));
```

```
    // remove members by index or by value
    myAL.remove(2);
    // print out the current size of the ArrayList
    System.out.println("List has " + myAL.size() + " items.");
  }
}
```

Listing 3.24 Using an ArrayList

The most important ArrayList methods are in bold font in Listing 3.24. Keep in mind that an ArrayList is actually a collection and not an actual array. You can't select members from an ArrayList using array-style square bracket syntax (e.g., myAL[2]); you have to use get() and add() instead.

Error Handling

An exception is a specific type of error generated by the system or your code. Both Java and J# use the same syntax for generating and trapping exceptions. In fact, the try-catch-finally blocks Java developers are familiar with are a common feature of all of the major .NET languages (J#, C#, VB.NET, and C++). In this section we will take a closer look at J# error-handling mechanisms.

Exceptions

In Java, all exceptions are descended from the java.lang.Exception class. In .NET, all exceptions are descended from the System.Exception class. J# supports *both* Java language exceptions and .NET Framework exceptions; which one is used depends on the code that threw the exception in the first place (that is, whether the code that caused the exception was a Java language class or a .NET Framework class).

All exceptions need to be caught somewhere. In one way, an exception is really a special case to the return statement rule. A method must return a valid value or *throw an exception* in order to exit. If a method returns an exception, the calling method then has to handle that exception or throw it up to the next level of calling code. An unhandled exception can actually bubble up from a deep method all the way through your application, causing the program to stop running. In summary:

1. A piece of code throws an exception, terminating the current method.
2. The parent method must catch the exception or throw it again, in which case the exception is passed up to the next level.
3. Eventually an uncaught exception will bubble all the way back up to the main() method used to start the program.

4. If the `main()` method does not catch and handle the exception, the Common Language Runtime catches it, exits the program, and displays the exception to the user.

Fortunately, the `try-catch-finally` block gives us a means to catch exceptions when they occur and deal with the issues immediately.

Try-catch-finally
The typical `try-catch-finally` block from Java works the same way in J#, as shown in Listing 3.25.

```
try
{
  // try some code that might throw an exception
}
catch (Exception e)
{
  // do something if an exception occurs
  // in this case, we're catching any generic Java Exception
}
finally
{
  // this code executes after everything else is done
  // we get here whether or not an exception was thrown
}
```

Listing 3.25 A `try-catch-finally` *block*

Note that in Listing 3.25, the generic `Exception` automatically refers to a `java.lang.Exception`. If you want to catch a generic .NET exception, you would need to use the line in Listing 3.26 instead.

```
catch (System.Exception e)
```

Listing 3.26 A generic .NET exception

Catching `java.lang.Exception` will *not* catch any .NET exceptions, but catching `System.Exception` *will* catch any Java exceptions. Every subclass of `java.lang.Exception` is automatically also a subclass of `System.Exception`. This means that although you can safely continue catching generic Java exceptions as you are used to, it might be worthwhile to get into the habit of catching the top-level .NET exception instead (using `System.Exception`), as this will ensure your exceptions will be caught whether they are thrown by J# or .NET classes.

Throwing Exceptions

At any time during your code, you can throw an exception using the throw keyword. This keyword allows a method to pass on an existing Exception (that is, send an exception the method has just received on up to the calling method) or create a new Exception (generate an entirely new exception and send it up to the calling method).

```
if(bankBalance < 100.00) {
  throw new LowBalanceException();
}
```

Listing 3.27 Throwing a new exception

When you add a throw statement, as in Listing 3.27, you trigger the normal exception-handling sequence of events:

1. The current function exits.
2. The exception linked to the throw keyword is passed up to the next layer of code (i.e., the code that called the current function).
3. The next layer must catch the exception or throw it up the chain.

Any method that contains a throw statement inside the method body must also contain the throws keyword in the method signature, indicating what exceptions the method can possibly produce. Listing 3.28 shows an example of a method that throws a customized exception (find out more about customized exceptions at ⇌JS030005).

```
public void doSomething(int x) throws myException
{
  if (x<=0)
    throw myException;
  else
  {
    // do something important
  }
}
```

Listing 3.28 Throwing an exception

In traditional Java, you must explicitly declare any exceptions that may be thrown from your code. In J#, you do not need to have a throws clause on your method declaration in order for it to throw a particular exception type.

As previously mentioned, J# supports both Java and .NET exception classes, and you are free to throw .NET exceptions in your own methods as well. If you're going to use your own custom exception, you need to make sure it implements the Throwable interface or extends an existing exception. See ⟲JS030005 for details on writing your own exceptions in J#.

Inheritance

Inheritance is a key part of object-oriented development and one of the primary concepts that drive the Java programming language. The primary purpose of inheritance is to allow reuse of code by allowing one class (the child or subclass) to inherit the variables and methods of another class (the base, parent, or superclass) and then extend upon the functionality of the parent class by adding new methods or modifying (*overriding*) some of the original ones. Code that is modified in a subclass will not affect the code of the base class.

The .NET Framework supports class inheritance in much the same way as Java (even cross-language), and J# code dealing with inheritance is exactly like that in Java.

Visibility

Before moving on to a discussion of inheritance coding in J#, we will first briefly review the concept of visibility. Every class, constructor, method, field, and variable definition may have a visibility keyword that restricts access rights to the class, constructor, method, field, or variable. These keywords also affect whether inherited methods, fields, and variables are accessible to subclasses.

- private   Visibility is limited to the current class only. Only methods within that class have access to its private members or methods. Inherited classes do *not* have direct access to private methods or variables in their parent class. The private keyword cannot be applied to constructors or classes.
- protected   Visibility is limited to the current class and classes that are derived from that class. Inherited classes can access protected members in their parent class, but unrelated classes cannot. This keyword cannot be applied to classes.
- package (default)   Visibility is limited to classes defined in the same package. The *package* in which a class resides is declared at the top of its file (e.g., package myPackage;) If the class is not part of a package, then the class can be seen only by other classes located in the same directory. The Java language does

not actually have a package visibility keyword. However, package-level visibility is assumed if no other visibility keyword is used. Note that in .NET, J# "packages" are actually treated as .NET namespaces behind the scenes; you'll learn all about the differences between packages and namespaces in the next topic of this chapter.
- public   Visibility is unrestricted. Every class has access.

Object-oriented designs must always account for visibility. In most cases, you will use either private or public.

Extending a Class
Extending a base class (*extend* is the Java language/J# syntax term for "inherit") is a very simple process involving a minor modification to the derived-class definition: simply add the extends keyword and the name of the base class. For example, to create a class that extends java.lang.Thread, use the code shown in Listing 3.29.

```
public class myThread extends Thread
{ }
```

Listing 3.29 Extending a class

The new class must have as much or more visibility than the base class. For example, if the base class is public, you cannot make the derived class protected.

This and Super
When you work with inheritance, it is often useful to be able to refer to the current object instance and the base class instance. The this keyword refers to the current class, and super refers to the base class. If, for example, an object instance needed to call the hello() method on the base class, you would use super.hello(), as shown in Listing 3.30.

```
public void derivedHello() {
  System.out.println("Hello from me.);
  System.out.println("And, hello from my base class: ");
  super.hello();
}
```

Listing 3.30 this and super

In many instances, you will want to use the super keyword to call a base class's method when overriding that method in a subclass. We'll touch on this again in the "Bugs and Caveats" section for this topic.

Override

When you override a method, you replace the parent class's functionality for that method. When a piece of code calls an overridden method in a child class, the method in the child class intercepts the call. The new method implementation can be completely different from the base class, but often it will also call the original superclass method, perhaps transforming the data along the way. Listing 3.31 shows a simple example of overriding a base class's method in a child class.

```
class MyBaseClass
{
  public void doSomething()
  {
    System.out.println("Superclasses are cool!");
  }
}

class MySubClass extends MyBaseClass
{
  public void doSomething()
  {
    // do something in the overridden method
    System.out.println("Subclasses are hot!");

    // now call the doSomething() method in MyBaseClass
    super.doSomething();
  }
}

public class myMainClass
{
  public static void main(String[] args)
  {
    MySubClass msc = new MySubClass();
    msc.doSomething();
  }
}
```

Listing 3.31 Overriding a method

MySubClass extends MyBaseClass and overrides its doSomething() method. In the overridden doSomething(), we output a message and then call the doSomething() method in MyBaseClass() using the super keyword.

If we compile and run the code in Listing 3.31, we get the output in Listing 3.32.

```
Subclasses are hot!
Superclasses are cool!
```

Listing 3.32 Output from Listing 3.31

Rules for Overriding a Method
In order to maintain object-oriented programming principles, .NET, like Java, forces you to follow some rules when you override a method:

1. The new method must have exactly the same return type and argument list as the superclass method. If the argument list changes, you are actually overloading a method instead of overriding it. An overloaded method shares the same method name, but has different arguments. An overloaded method is entirely separate from the base class method. We'll cover overloaded methods later in this section.
2. The new method must have the same or greater visibility than the superclass method. In other words, if the superclass method is `public`, the new method must also be `public`. However, if the superclass method is `package`, the new method can be `protected` or `public`. The order of visibility (from least to most) is `private`, `package`, `protected`, then `public`.
3. The new method can throw fewer checked exceptions than the superclass method, but not more. For example, if the superclass method doesn't throw any exceptions, the new method can't throw any, either.
4. The method can throw subclasses of the exceptions thrown by the superclass method, but not superclasses of those exceptions. For example, if the base class method throws `IOException`, the subclass can throw `ConnectIOException` (a subclass of `IOException`) in place of `IOException`. However, the subclass method cannot throw `Exception` (a more general exception) in place of `IOException`.

Rules 2 through 4 are particularly important and relate to something known as the Liskov Substitution Principle: any subclass must be interchangeable with its superclass. In other words, if you write code that works with the superclass, it should also work with any subclass. Note that the inverse statement isn't necessarily true. In fact, you should be able to write code specifically for the subclass; otherwise, the subclass isn't really useful.

Constructors and Inheritance

When you inherit from a base class, you must remember that the subclass inherits the constructor of the base class, in addition to the base class's regular methods. When you create an instance of a subclass, the constructor for its base class is called *first,* and then the subclass's own constructor is called. For example, when we create an instance of My-SubClass in Listing 3.31, the CLR actually starts off by creating an instance of MyBaseClass behind the scenes and running the MyBaseClass() constructor. It then creates an instance of MySubClass and runs the My-SubClass() constructor. (Note that in the case of Listing 3.31, however, both MyBaseClass and MySubClass had default—that is to say, empty—constructors that don't do anything.) Again, constructors are always called in order of inheritance, from the top down.

One more thing to note about constructors and inheritance is that if your class has a constructor that accepts an argument, you will not be able to pass the argument back up to the base class. Worse yet, if your base class has a constructor with an argument, but does not have a no-argument constructor, the compiler will not let you create an instance of your derived class! To work around these problems, you can preempt the CLR call to the base class constructor by using the super() constructor. The super() constructor call must be the very first line inside your derived class's constructor body. Consider the code in Listing 3.33.

```
class Instrument {
  Instrument() {
  System.out.println("Instrument Constructor");
  }
}

class Guitar extends Instrument {
  Guitar(int i) {
    System.out.println("Guitar -" + i + " constructor");
  }
}

public class ElectricGuitar extends Guitar {
  ElectricGuitar() {
    super(5);
    System.out.println("ElectricGuitar constructor");
  }
```

```
    public static void main(String[] args) {
        ElectricGuitar e = new ElectricGuitar();
    }
}
```

Listing 3.33 Constructor chains

Because Guitar requires an integer, we must pass an integer using the super() constructor. However, Instrument still has a no-argument constructor, so the Guitar class does not have to call super() explicitly. The constructor for ElectricGuitar, on the other hand, must explicitly call the constructor for Guitar, as Guitar doesn't have a default constructor. If we left out the bold line in Listing 3.33, our program wouldn't compile.

Overloading Methods
When you overload a method, you provide alternative functionality based on different method arguments and return values. You can overload methods defined in your own class or methods defined in a base class. In order for the CLR to differentiate between overloaded methods, each method must have a unique list of arguments. Simply having a different return type is not enough, because you can call a method while ignoring the return type (e.g., String s = f(); versus simply f();). Listing 3.34 illustrates a typical set of examples.

```
public void hello() {
    System.out.println("Hello Guest");
}
public void hello(String name) {
    System.out.println("Hello " + name);
}
public String hello(int number) {
    return ("Hello number " + number);
}
```

Listing 3.34 Overloading methods

Surprisingly, simply switching the order of arguments is enough to guarantee uniqueness. However, you should avoid overloading methods by switching the argument order, as it creates methods that easily confuse other developers.

EXAMPLE

We will take one of the classic examples for illustrating inheritance in a Java application and recreate it in J#. We will start by creating a simple

`Calculator` class that knows how to perform addition and subtraction operations. Then we will create a specialized `ScientificCalculator` subclass by extending `Calculator`. Over the course of this example, you'll see many instances of the basic J# syntax we examined throughout this topic.

The Calculator Base Class

Begin by opening Visual Studio .NET and clicking the **New Project** button. Choose the Visual J# console application template. Give your application a name other than `ConsoleApplication1`—for this example, we'll call ours `Calculator`. Click **OK,** and Visual Studio .NET will set up a new solution and project (both called `Calculator`), and provide a default class file called `Class1.jsl`, as shown in Figure 3.1. Since `Class1.jsl` already has an empty `main()` method in it (automatically generated by VS .NET) and is set up as the starting class for the application, we're going to use it to drive our application. Before we do that, however, we first need to create our `Calculator` class.

Right-click on **Calculator** (not **Solution 'Calculator'**) in the Solution Explorer and select **Add → Add New Item.** Choose **Visual J# Class** from the available templates, name it `Calculator.jsl`, and click **Open.** A new file will be added to the Solution Explorer, and the code for `Calculator.jsl` will appear in your Design window, as shown in Figure 3.3.

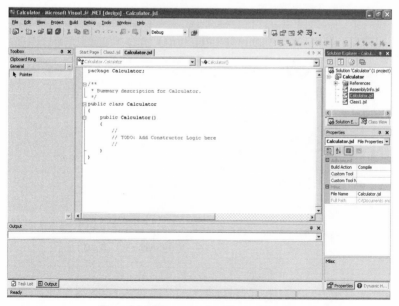

Figure 3.3 Adding a new class file to a J# project

As you can see in Figure 3.3, Visual Studio .NET automatically adds some basic code to a newly created class, including a package declaration (packages are discussed further in the next topic of this chapter), a public class declaration, and a basic no-argument constructor (Calculator()). Our Calculator class is simple enough that we don't really need a constructor, so let's leave the constructor empty for now and add some functionality to our Calculator class.

The Base Class Methods
Inside the Calculator class, add two new methods, as shown in Listing 3.35.

```
public class Calculator
{
  public int add(int a, int b) { return a + b; }
  public int subtract(int a, int b) {return a - b; }
}
```

Listing 3.35 Calculator *class*

These two methods will allow the calculator to add and subtract integers. Now, double-click on Class1.jsl in the Solution Explorer, and add the code in Listing 3.36 to the main() method (you can remove the autogenerated comments from inside main() first, although it is not necessary).

```
public static void main(String[] args)
{
  Calculator myCalc = new Calculator();
  try
  {
    int a = Integer.parseInt(args[0]);
    int b = Integer.parseInt(args[2]);
    char op = args[1].charAt(0);

    switch (op)
    {
      case '+':
        System.out.println(a + " " + op + " " + b +
                           " = " + myCalc.add(a,b));
        break;
      case '-':
        System.out.println(a + " " + op + " " + b +
```

```
                              " = " + myCalc.subtract(a,b));
      break;
   default:
      System.out.println("Sorry, invalid operator.");
  };
}
catch (IndexOutOfBoundsException e)
{
   System.out.println(
      "Please use the format: Calculator a [+/-] b");
}
catch (NumberFormatException e)
{
   System.out.println(
      "Please use the format: Calculator a [+/-] b");
}
}
```

Listing 3.36 A main() *method for our* Calculator *class*

Our main() method accepts three parameters from the command line and will give an error message if the user enters less than three (we catch an IndexOutOfBoundsException to handle the case of too few parameters). The first and third parameters to main() are the numbers we will be adding or subtracting. All parameters on the command line are initially treated as strings, so we need to use a special method called Integer.parseInt() to convert our strings to integers. Similarly, we need to use the String.charAt() method to convert the second main() argument to a character. We convert it to a char so we can use it as a control for our switch statement (switch statements, you may remember, must be ordinal). You can find more information on parseInt(), charAt(), and other useful type conversion methods at ☞JS030006.

Compiling and Testing the Base Class

Our basic calculator program is now ready to try out. Compile it to an MSIL executable assembly by selecting **Build Calculator** from the Build menu. Now, open a Visual Studio .NET Command Prompt and switch to the directory in which your application was built. By default, the directory in which you will find your compiled application will be My Documents\Visual Studio Projects\Calculator\bin\debug. In this directory, you'll find a file named Calculator.exe—this is your compiled Calculator application.

Try running `Calculator.exe` as shown in Listing 3.43.

```
C:\>Calculator 1 + 1
1 + 1 = 2

C:\>Calculator 892 - 384
892 - 384 = 508

C:\>Calculator foo - 93
Please use the format: Calculator a [+/-] b

C:\>Calculator 2 -
Please use the format: Calculator a [+/-] b
```

Listing 3.37 Output from `Calculator` *base class*

It looks like our `Calculator` class is functioning correctly and handling errors as we've designed it to. Now we will try extending it to create a more complex calculator.

The ScientificCalculator Class

We are now going to extend (that is, create a new class that inherits from) the `Calculator` class and add a new method for calculating factorials. Right-click on the Calculator project in your Solution Explorer and select **Add → Add New Item.** Select a J# Class template again, and name it `ScientificCalculator.jsl`. Click **OK** to add yet another new class file to your Solution Explorer. Again, we don't need to worry about the generated constructor method (`ScientificCalculator()`) or the `package` statement. However, we do need to make a change to the class declaration itself. We need to modify it so that `ScientificCalculator` extends our base `Calculator` class as shown in Listing 3.38 (code you need to add is in bold).

```
public class ScientificCalculator extends Calculator
```

Listing 3.38 Extending `Calculator`

Because `ScientificCalculator` is inheriting from `Calculator`, the `add()` and `subtract()` methods we designed in Listing 3.35 will now be available to `ScientificCalculator`. Now we will add a new method called `factorial()` that will calculate the product of all numbers from 1 to an integer a specified as a parameter. The code for the `factorial()` method, which you should add to your `ScientificCalculator` class, is shown in Listing 3.39.

```
public class ScientificCalculator extends Calculator
{
  public int factorial(int a)
  {
    for (int n = a - 1; n > 1; n --)
    {
      a *= n;
    }
    return a;
  }
}
```

Listing 3.39 The factorial() *method*

We use a simple for loop to find the product. Note that a *= n is a short-cut that means the same as a = a * n.

Obviously, we also need to make a few changes to our main() method in Class1.jsl in order to have it work with ScientificCalculator instead of Calculator. These changes are highlighted in Listing 3.40.

```
public static void main(String[] args)
{
  ScientificCalculator myCalc = new ScientificCalculator();
  try
  {
    int a = Integer.parseInt(args[0]);
    int b = 0;
    char op = args[1].charAt(0);

    // we use the ! character to represent factorial
    if (op != '!')
      b = Integer.parseInt(args[2]);

    switch (op)
    {
      case '+':
        System.out.println(a + " " + op + " " + b +
                           " = " + myCalc.add(a,b));
        break;
      case '-':
        System.out.println(a + " " + op + " " + b +
                           " = " + myCalc.subtract(a,b));
```

```
      break;
  case '!':
    System.out.println(a + " " + op + " = " +
                    myCalc.factorial(a));
      break;
    default:
      System.out.println("Sorry, invalid operator.");
  };
}
// catch statements are identical - removed for brevity
}
```

Listing 3.40 Using `ScientificCalculator`

One important change is that we now have to account for the possibility that there will be only two command-line parameters (an integer and an operator) instead of three, since the `factorial()` method requires only one integer, not two. We do this by using an `if` statement to assign a value to `b` only if the operator is not `'!'` (factorial). We also must add an additional `case` to the `switch` statement to handle the `'!'` operator.

Compiling and Running the Derived Class
Compile your application as before by selecting **Build → Build Solution.** Return to the directory in which your application compiles (most likely, `My Documents\Visual Studio Projects\Calculator\bin\debug`) and try running it with the same commands as in Listing 3.37. You will find that the + and - operators still work just as they did before. In addition, however, you will also be able to use the ! operator to perform a factorial operation, as shown in Listing 3.41.

```
C:\>Calculator 5 !
5 ! = 120
```

Listing 3.41 Using `factorial()`

You can find downloadable source code for this example at ◦**CN**⟩JS030007.

HOW AND WHY

How Can I Add Special Characters to Strings in J#?
Some characters, such as tabs, linefeeds, and carriage returns, cannot be represented in a string by a single keyboard character. In J#, as in the Java language, these characters can be used in strings by entering a spe-

cial *escape code,* which takes the form of a backslash character ("\") followed by a letter. For example, you can add a newline character (i.e., a line break) to a string using \n or a tab character using \t. You can find more information on and examples of special escape characters in J# strings at ᵒᶜ͍⟩JS030008.

BUGS AND CAVEATS

Calling Base Class Methods

When you override a base class method, you should take care to always call the base class method using super and the base method. If you do not, you take the risk of accidentally skipping critical code. For example, the base class may set some critical field. If you don't either duplicate the code or call the base method using super, the data might not get stored correctly. For an example, see ᵒᶜ͍⟩JS030009.

DESIGN NOTES

Some Tricky Loop Conditions

With all three types of loop (for, while, and do-while), you can actually use any function that will return a Boolean value as the condition. Boolean values are generated by any equality statement (e.g., ==, >,<), as well as many methods. The code in Listing 3.42, for example, is a valid way to loop through every element in an ArrayList.

```
// assumes myList is a filled ArrayList
Iterator myIt = myList.iterator();
while (myIt.hasNext()) {
  Object o = myList.next();
}
```

Listing 3.42 Using a loop to iterate an ArrayList

The hasNext() method returns a Boolean value that acts as the condition for continuing our loop.

SUMMARY

Basic J# syntax is identical to basic Java language syntax. Variables and arrays can be declared and instantiated as though they were Java data types, even though the underlying types are actually .NET types (as we will see in the next topic). Looping can be controlled with for, while, and do-while statements. Decision making can be controlled via if/else blocks and switch statements. Exceptions can be thrown using the throws statement and handled using try-catch-finally blocks, with a catch block for each possible exception that could occur. Classes can inherit from one another using the extends keyword, and methods can be overridden or overloaded simply by redeclaring them in a derived class.

Now that you know that you can use your Java skills comfortably in J#, the next topic of this chapter will examine some of the extended features of J# provided by the BCL. We will demonstrate that what's happening "under the hood" in J# is really quite a bit different from what goes on in Java.

Topic: J# and the Base Class Library (BCL)

As we saw in the preceding topic, J# provides all of the same features and syntax as the Java language. However, J# actually consists of an independently developed set of libraries created with the sole intention of recreating a subset of the JDK as accurately as possible under the .NET Framework. One positive feature of J# is that it not only has access to the JDK Library functionality with which you are so familiar but also has full access to the much larger, more diverse libraries included with the .NET Framework. As we will see in this topic, and throughout the rest of this CodeNotes, the .NET Framework Libraries have many similarities with the JDK libraries, but there are some significant differences (which we will discuss in this topic) and some major enhancements.

The .NET Framework includes an enormous collection of managed classes that are usable by any language supported by the Common Language Runtime (CLR). This single Framework is accessible to developers using VB.NET, Managed C++, C#, and, of course, J#, among many other languages. The Framework classes provide everything you will need to access all of .NET's features, from standard data types to complex interoperability features. Some of the more interesting areas of the Framework (many of which are examined in this book) are as follows:

- Fundamentals and common data types (covered in the preceding topic)
- Complex data types such as collections, hashtables, and lists
- File I/O (input/output) classes

- Forms design and GDI interface classes (Chapter 4)
- Networking and Web access classes
- Web Forms and ASP.NET-related classes (Chapter 5)
- XML parsing and generating
- Windows OS access

All of the classes in the Framework are organized into *namespaces.* Namespaces are like packages in Java; they represent hierarchical groups of classes sorted by functionality. Namespaces help prevent name collisions between classes by providing a hierarchy. Namespaces also simplify access to the Framework in that they allow you to include just the classes you need in your compiled assemblies. You can find a complete list of the .NET Framework namespaces at ⌀ᶜᴺJS030016.

When you use the `import` statement in J#, you are actually referencing .NET namespaces rather than Java packages from the Java core libraries (we'll see more about Java packages and .NET namespaces later in this topic). However, Microsoft has mirrored much of the JDK functionality so seamlessly in J# that you'll never know the difference—in most cases, you can continue to import the same Java classes you are used to. Behind the scenes, however, many of the familiar JDK classes have been replaced by or mapped to .NET classes to allow better interaction within the .NET Framework.

CONCEPTS

java.lang.Object versus System.Object

In Java, every nonprimitive data type derives from the ultimate base class, `java.lang.Object` (we'll discuss the concept of primitive versus nonprimitive data types subsequently). In .NET (and therefore in J#), *every* data type derives from the `System.Object` class. In order to avoid any conflicts, and in order to allow Java code to compile under .NET, `java.lang.Object` is an alias for `System.Object` in J#. This means that no matter which one you refer to in your code, you're still actually referring to the same class, which is ultimately `System.Object`.

The `java.lang.Object` class does have a number of methods that do not exist in the `System.Object` class (remember, `System.Object` existed in the .NET Framework long before J# was created). When your J# code calls these methods, the calls are redirected to a special class called `com.ms.vjsharp.lang.ObjectImpl`, whose sole purpose is to support the base `java.lang.Object` methods that don't exist (at least in the same place) in .NET. Once again, however, you don't have to worry about which class you're actually calling methods on, because the process happens entirely behind the scenes.

The Object Life Cycle

The life cycle of an object in the CLR is very similar to the life cycle of an object in the JVM. The basic phases in a J# object's life are as follows:

1. All objects are instances of a class. This class is like a blueprint, and you can create as many objects of the same type as you like from a single blueprint. In general, you create an instance of a class (a.k.a. an object) with a line of code as shown in Listing 3.43.

```
MyObject myObjectInstance = new MyObject();
```

Listing 3.43 Instantiating a class

Listing 3.43 is actually doing three things:

a. The code `MyObject myObjectInstance` *declares* that the variable `myObjectInstance` will refer to an object of type `MyObject`. The object does not actually exist yet, because no space has been allocated for it.

b. The `new` operator *instantiates* an object by allocating space for it on the heap (the heap is an area of memory set aside specifically for objects). You don't have to instantiate an object right away, but you won't be able to use it until you do (because, as we've said, it doesn't exist yet).

c. Calling `MyObject()` *initializes* the object by calling its constructor. The constructor assigns values to any necessary initial data that the object will require when it is used. In Listing 3.43 we're calling a constructor that has no parameters. This constructor may or may not exist in the code for the class. If the constructor doesn't exist, the CLR will simply use a default empty constructor that does nothing. We could also have initialized `myObjectInstance` by calling a constructor with parameters, if one existed in the class.

Remember that all nonprimitive variables are simply references to a memory location where information about the object is stored. This means that if a class has a constructor that takes an object as a parameter (as opposed to a primitive), you're not sending that constructor a new object—you're simply sending it a reference to an object that already exists.

2. Once an object has been created, you can do two things with it:
   a. If it has `public` variables, you can read or write their values, referencing them with the form `myObjectInstance.myVariable`. The dot-operator (".") indicates that what comes after the dot is contained within what came before it. Note that, in general, it is not advisable to have global `public` variables that can be accessed from other classes—it is much safer to use global `private` variables and create *accessor methods,* whose sole purpose is to manipulate variables within an object without allowing foreign classes to change them directly.
   b. If an object has methods, you can call these methods. An object call looks like this: `myObjectInstance.myMethod(parameters)`. The parameters of a method can be literals (e.g., "5" is a literal integer) or variables (primitives or objects), depending on what is required by the method code. Note that when you create an instance of a class (a new object) only the methods in that class that were declared `public` will be available to you.

3. When your code is finished with an object (i.e., there are no more references to it), it becomes eligible for *garbage collection.* In general, references to objects will disappear when the object goes out of scope (that is, when the block of code in which the object variable was instantiated is complete). The garbage collector in the CLR periodically checks for objects that no longer have any references to them and frees up the memory that was allocated to these objects. You don't usually have control over when or how the garbage collector runs, although manual activation of it is possible (⌐**CN**JS030010).

   It is also possible to define a block of code that will always execute immediately before an object is garbage-collected. Every .NET object has a `finalize()` method that is defined in the `System.Object` class from which all other classes are derived. In certain cases, it is necessary to override this method when writing your own classes. See ⌐**CN**JS030011 for more details.

Object life cycles in Java (under the JVM) and in J# (under the CLR) are quite similar, even under the hood. However, as you will see in the next section, there is some difference in how Java and J# handle primitives (i.e., nonObject data types).

Primitives

Java makes a distinction between objects (which encompass most data types) and primitive types. The primary difference between objects and primitives is that objects are created on the heap (after you instantiate them using new) and primitives are created on the stack. The heap and the stack are just two different memory areas that are accessed in slightly different fashions. The stack is generally considered more transient and usually holds less data. Primitive types are all "simple" data types, such as integers, Booleans, floats, and doubles, and are not subject to garbage collection or any of the other advantages of more complex object data types.

.NET handles primitives a bit differently than Java. Instead of simply having these data types built into the CLR, .NET actually defines primitives as structures in the System namespace in the .NET Framework. Structures are like classes, except that they are placed on the stack instead of the heap (and therefore memory for them is allocated differently). All .NET languages have their own way of creating an instance of these "primitive" structures. In J#, you use the int keyword. In Visual Basic .NET, you use Integer. In either case, what you're actually getting is an instance of the object System.Int32 (a 32-bit integer). Although in Java you still have to wrap primitive types in objects in order to treat them as objects (e.g., new Integer(38) is an Integer object wrapping an int primitive), other .NET languages allow you to treat primitives as objects and do all the wrapping behind the scenes. Once again, for most purposes, this difference between how Java and J# handle primitives will have little or no effect on your code.

Value Types

Arguments can be passed into and out of functions in two different ways: by value or by reference. In Java, you don't have a choice about how your data is passed—the JVM automatically decides, depending on the data type, which way to pass it. In general, primitive data types get passed by value and all others get passed by reference.

.NET also makes a distinction between value types and reference types. Unlike Java, however, many .NET languages allow you to define your own value types. That is, you can create a data type that will always be passed by value or by reference. Other .NET languages, such as C# and VB.NET, support code that allows you to define value types. However, since Java does not support this functionality, neither does J#.

Even though you can't define new value types using J#, you can take advantage of some previously existing value types defined within the .NET Framework that are not available to ordinary Java developers. A good example of an existing value data type in .NET is an *enumeration,* which is a set of named constants. (Please don't confuse the .NET enumeration data type with the java.util.Enumeration class. The Enumeration class serves an entirely different function related to collections.)

Enumerations are useful for when you have a variable that has a specific set of values that can be assigned to it. You can't define your own enumerations, but you can use existing ones, such as the DayOfWeek enumeration demonstrated in Listing 3.44.

```
System.DayOfWeek myDay = new System.DayOfWeek();
myDay = System.DayOfWeek.Sunday;
while ((int)myDay < 7)
{
   System.out.println("I don't like " + myDay + "s.");
   myDay++;
}
```

Listing 3.44 Using the DayOfWeek enumeration

As you can see, enumeration constants are represented as integers, can be cast back and forth from integers, and can have arithmetic operations performed on them. Thus, the output of the code in Listing 3.44 will look like that in Listing 3.45.

```
I don't like Sundays.
I don't like Mondays.
I don't like Tuesdays.
I don't like Wednesdays.
I don't like Thursdays.
I don't like Fridays.
I don't like Saturdays.
```

Listing 3.45 Output from Listing 3.44

Although many of the new classes supported by J# are extensions on Java in order to take advantage of .NET technologies (and will be covered in the rest of this CodeNotes), there are several other examples of useful .NET classes for everyday programming that Microsoft has allowed into the J# specification. For information on some of these, please see JS030012.

Interfaces

An *interface* is like a class that declares methods but doesn't implement any of them. Other classes can then implement interfaces and must provide bodies for all the declared methods as well. Interfaces are like templates for classes—they dictate structure but leave the actual content up to the class designer.

Both Java and J# support interfaces in the same way. Listings 3.46 and 3.47 show an example of a very simple interface and a class that implements it.

```
public interface iMyInterface
{
  void doSomething();
}
```

Listing 3.46 Creating an interface

```
public class MyClass implements iMyInterface
{
  public void doSomething()
  {
    // must add code here to implement the doSomething method
  }
}
```

Listing 3.47 Implementing an interface

As you can see, a class that implements an interface must implement all methods defined in the interface, but the class can change the visibility modifiers of those methods (public, private, etc.). The class can also add a throws clause to a method to have it throw an exception, even if the method in the interface does not declare the exception. One thing you *cannot* do, however, is change the number or data type of parameters to a method declared in the interface. In Listing 3.47, we could have declared a doSomething(int myInt) method *in addition* to the doSomething() with no arguments (this is called *overloading*), but we couldn't leave the doSomething() method out altogether without producing a compilation error.

One additional feature of J# in terms of interfaces is that J# classes can implement interfaces that were written in *other languages*. Because everything in .NET is eventually compiled to MSIL, you could write an interface in C# (or VB.NET or Managed C++), and then implement it in a J# class with no special code required. Similarly, you could write an interface in J# and then implement it in any other .NET language. This means that the preexisting interfaces that ship with .NET can be used by any language, including J#, and you don't have to worry about converting them from the language in which they were originally written.

Packages versus Namespaces

In Java, classes are often arranged into *packages*. A package is basically a collection of classes with similar functionality that are grouped together for convenience. Packages can be nested within one another in order to create a hierarchy of related classes, usually ranging from the most general functionality in the root packages to very specific functionality in deeply nested packages.

You can indicate what package a class (or classes) will be in by using the package statement at the top of the class file, as shown in Listing 3.48.

```
package codenotes;

class MyClass
{
    // class contents
}
```

Listing 3.48 Using the package statement

MyClass is in a package named codenotes. MyClass, and any other classes that appear in the same file can be referred to from other classes using a qualified name like codenotes.MyClass. Similarly, its methods can be called by referring to codenotes.MyClass.myMethod().

In Java, when you put a class in a package, you must also adjust your directory structure to match that of your package hierarchy. That means that the file that contains MyClass would have to be located in a directory called codenotes underneath the root directory of your application. If we created another class named MyOtherClass and specified that it was in the package codenotes.utils, its file would have to be placed in the codenotes\utils directory in order for it to compile correctly using the Java compiler (javac.exe).

For an example of an existing set of packages, we need look no further than the JDK. All of the classes in the Java core libraries are contained within a package called java, which in turn contains other packages like java.lang, java.math, java.text, and so on. The java.lang and java.system packages are available implicitly in any new class. However, you must explicitly include any other packages using the import statement, as shown in Listing 3.49.

```
import java.text.*;
import java.math.*;
import codenotes.MyClass;
```

Listing 3.49 Importing packages

Using the * wildcard allows you to import every class in a particular package. You can also import specific classes from a package by replacing the wildcard character with the name of the package. Although it can increase the length of your code to import every class independently, it is often better to explicitly import each required class, as importing entire packages from various sources can cause name conflicts later if you are not careful. For example, both the core Java packages java.util.* and java.awt.* (used for graphics in traditional Java) have a class called List; if you imported both of these and then tried to create a List object in your code, the compiler would not know which List you were referring to.

Namespaces

.NET uses *namespaces* instead of packages. The primary difference between a namespace and a package is that namespaces are virtual; that is, there's no need to mimic the namespace hierarchy in a directory structure. To the developer, however, both namespaces and packages serve exactly the same purpose within an application (they represent groups of classes with related functionality). In addition, in order to maintain Java language syntax, Microsoft has mapped the package and import statements so that each will function in J# just as they do in Java, even though they are actually creating and importing namespaces (not packages) behind the scenes.

So why is it important that we distinguish between packages and namespaces? It turns out that it makes a difference in terms of application deployment. We'll take a look at how the distinction between packages and namespaces affects deployment in the next section of this topic.

JARs versus Assemblies

A typical Java library will consist of a large collection of class files arranged in a directory structure that mimics the package structure dictated inside the class code. This is, however, an inconvenient way of distributing your application to users. In order to allow large quantities of classes to be *deployed* (that is, packaged and distributed to users) as a single file, Java developers use a special compressed format called a Java Archive, or JAR.

To create a JAR file, you open a command prompt and change to the root directory of your Java files (e.g., the one below which all your packages are arranged in the correct directory structures). The command in Listing 3.50 will create a file named myApplication.jar.

```
jar -cf myApplication.jar *.*
```

Listing 3.50 Creating a JAR file

The two command-line options are used to indicate that we're creating a new archive (c), and that we want to explicitly specify an archive file name (f). Note that files other than compiled .class files can also be included in a JAR. The JAR file will maintain the directory structure your library had in its expanded form.

Once you have a JAR file, it is typically referenced in your machine's CLASSPATH environment variable so that it is accessible to other Java applications. Java applications can then import classes from the JAR file using the import statement as usual. (You can find more information on using the CLASSPATH variable with Java JARs at ⟲JS030013.) When the JVM is running a Java application and finds a referenced package name it doesn't recognize, the first place the compiler looks is in the CLASSPATH to see whether there are any referenced JARs that contain the appropriate package. Using JARs, large amounts of classes can be moved from place to place and maintained on a machine in a single file instead of a large, complex directory structure.

Assemblies
.NET does *not* use the CLASSPATH, and J# does not know how to read JAR files, which contain compiled Java (not J#) bytecode. Instead, as previously mentioned, J# code is compiled into *assemblies* that contain generic MSIL code, which can later be interpreted by the CLR at runtime. Namespaces and classes in an assembly can be imported into another application just like the packages and classes in a JAR can. The difference is that imported assemblies must be specified to the .NET compiler at runtime—it doesn't automatically know where to look for them.

Visual Studio .NET makes adding an assembly reference easy by providing a GUI interface for it via the Project menu. We'll look at how to use this interface in the "Example" section at the end of this topic. For now, understand that you reference each assembly you want to use in your application by selecting it from a menu. You can then use the import statement in your J# code to import the various namespaces contained within a referenced assembly. The code contained within any imported namespaces will then be available to your new code as though it were a part of your application. Alternatively, you can reference classes in imported assemblies using their fully qualified names (e.g., `MyNamespace.MyClass.myMethod()`).

Note that .NET applications can be further optimized for deployment by compiling them into Microsoft Installer (MSI) format. For more information on MSI, please see ᴐᴺ᷎JS030014.

EXAMPLE

In this example we're going to build on our previous `Calculator` and `ScientificCalculator` examples from the first topic. We'll show how these classes can be compiled into a class library assembly (DLL). We will then import the assembly into another application and access its classes and methods.

Start by opening Visual Studio .NET and clicking on the **New Project** button. Choose the **J# Class Library** template, name your project `MathLib`, and click the **OK** button to begin. Visual Studio will set up a new class library solution and project for you. Remember that a class library is compiled into a .DLL file instead of an .EXE. This means that it will not have a `main()` method and cannot be "run" as an independent application. A class library is meant to be a collection of classes that can be imported and used in other applications.

Visual Studio .NET will create a default class file named `Class1.jsl`. For the sake of simplicity, we'll make use of this class file instead of adding our own. Click on `Class1.jsl` to open it in the Code window and remove everything in it except for the first line: `package MathLib;`. We need this line to provide a namespace for our classes so that we can reference them from elsewhere.

Add the code from Listing 3.35 (`Calculator`) and Listing 3.38 (`ScientificCalculator`) to `Class1.jsl` so that it looks like Listing 3.51.

```
package MathLib;

public class Calculator
{
  public int add(int a, int b) { return a + b; }
  public int subtract (int a, int b) {return a - b; }
}

public class ScientificCalculator extends Calculator
```

```
{
  public int factorial (int a)
  {
    for (int n = a - 1; n > 1; n --)
    {
      a *= n;
    }
    return a;
  }
}
```

Listing 3.51 The `MathLib` *class library*

Note that, as mentioned in the "Core Concepts" section of this chapter, it is perfectly acceptable to have multiple public J# classes in a single `.jsl` file. To compile your application, select **Build Solution** from the Build menu. Compiling the application will create a file named `MathLib.dll` in your `MathLib\bin\debug` directory. `MathLib.dll` is your class library, and we're now going to import it into another application.

Select **New → Project** from the File menu. This time, choose to create a new J# console application and name it `MyCalculator`. Make sure the **Close Solution** radio button is selected (not **Add to Solution**), and click the **OK** button to create the new project. As in the example in the preceding topic, Visual Studio .NET will generate the necessary files for a console application, including an empty class file named `Class1.jsl`.

Before we do anything else, we need to create a *reference* to `MathLib.dll` from our new application. Select **Add Reference** from the Project menu and a new Add Reference window will open. Click the **Browse** button, and locate and select `MathLib.dll` (remember that it will be located in the `MathLib\bin\debug` folder on your hard drive). It should appear in the Selected Components box, as shown in Figure 3.4. After you select `MathLib.dll`, click **OK** to return to your application. `MathLib` should now be visible under the References heading in your Solution Explorer.

In `Class1.jsl`, insert the code found in Listing 3.40 from our original example into the `main()` method. Since we're really accessing the same classes, all the same code should work. However, if you try compiling your application now, it won't work. Why? Because even though we created a reference to `MathLib.dll` in our solution, `Class1` itself still doesn't know how to find the `ScientificCalculator` class (or any other class in `MathLib` for that matter). We need to import the `MathLib` namespace into our class file. Add the line shown in Listing 3.52 to `Class1.jsl`, just below the `package` declaration.

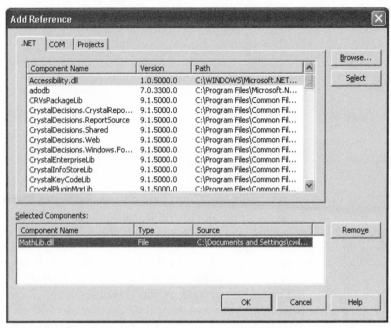

Figure 3.4 Adding a reference to `MathLib.dll`

```
import MathLib.ScientificCalculator;
```

Listing 3.52 Importing `MathLib`

In Listing 3.52, we're importing only the `ScientificCalculator` class because that's all we need. We could also have imported `MathLib.*` if we planned to use all the classes contained within the `MathLib` namespace.

Now compile your application (by going to **Build → Build Solution**). `MyCalculator.exe` will be created in the `MyCalculator\bin\debug` directory. Open a .NET Command Prompt and try running `MyCalculator.exe`, and you will see that it behaves exactly as the first example in this chapter did.

When you import an assembly into an application, you can do more than just import its namespaces and call its methods. If it contains interfaces, you can implement those interfaces. You can also define new classes in your application that extend the ones in the imported assembly. Class library assemblies are a great way of keeping collections of classes together in a single file and distributing them for use in other applications, without ever having to rewrite any code.

BUGS AND CAVEATS

Restrictions of the J# Language
Because J# was designed to follow Java language syntax so carefully, there are certain things that can be done in other .NET languages that are not possible in J#. Specifically, this includes defining new properties, events, value types, and delegates. We mentioned value types earlier in this chapter, and we'll talk about delegates in Chapter 4. For brief definitions of each of these items and explanations of how their absence from J# will affect your programming, please see ⬦JS030015.

DESIGN NOTES

Debug versus Release Mode
In all the examples in this chapter (and for the rest of this CodeNotes), we compiled our assemblies in Debug mode. When in Debug mode, .NET generates assemblies that contain not only the code you've written converted into IL, but also a great deal of additional IL code that is used by the CLR for debugging purposes. This is also why all of our compiled applications have ended up in the bin\debug directory.

When your application is bugfree and you are ready to release it to the public, you would typically compile it in Release mode instead. Switching to Release mode is extremely simple. Simply select Release, instead of Debug, from the drop-down menu located on the toolbar at the top of your VS .NET window (Figure 3.5).

Generally, assemblies compiled in Release mode will be smaller than assemblies compiled in Debug mode, since they will not contain any of the extra debugging code. You will find assemblies compiled in Release mode in your application's bin\release directory.

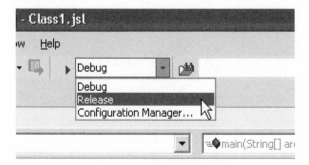

Figure 3.5 Switching to Release mode

Using ILDASM

ILDASM.EXE is a tool that is included with the .NET Framework SDK and Visual Studio .NET. It allows you to investigate the contents of compiled .NET assemblies (all of which, of course, are made up of IL code). You can use ILDASM.EXE to see what classes are included in a compiled assembly and what constructors and methods those classes support. For more information on ILDASM.EXE, please see ⚙JS010001.

SUMMARY

J# provides Java language developers with a familiar syntax and set of JDK functionality while also allowing them to take full advantage of all the additional features of the .NET Framework. In addition, because all .NET languages share the Framework and run against the Common Language Runtime, classes and interfaces written in one language can be easily implemented and extended in another language.

Although J# looks like Java on the face of it, there are some significant differences between how various data types are implemented in the .NET Framework and how they were implemented in the JDK core libraries. Primitives are special cases in Java, but in J# they are actually just structures defined within the System namespace and fall into the category of value types. Although other languages allow you to define your own value types, J# (in keeping with Java language syntax) does not—but you can still take advantage of any of the built-in value types in the .NET Framework.

Everything in the Framework and most of the classes you will create yourself are organized into namespaces. Namespaces in .NET are analogous to packages in Java. The main difference between the two shows up during the deployment phase of your application. In Java, packages are compressed into JAR files and the JAR files are referenced in your machine's CLASSPATH variable. The JVM knows to examine the CLASSPATH if it does not recognize an imported package or class. In .NET, you compile your classes into assemblies that must be imported into your application at compile time (although VS .NET lets you set up your solution so this happens automatically).

Chapter Summary

This chapter solidifies the concept that J# is virtually identical to Java on the surface, but that something different is going on behind the scenes when you compile a J# application to an MSIL assembly. You can program J# applications as though you were writing Java, and chances are (for basic tasks), you will never know the difference. The real benefits of J# become clear when you start to take advantage of classes in the .NET Framework to create Windows Forms, interact with databases, or create online applications, all of which will be discussed in the remainder of this book.

Once again, you can still use much of the Java you know and leverage the thousands of classes in the .NET Framework, take advantage of the rapid application development environment provided by VS .NET, and work seamlessly with other .NET languages such as C# and VB.NET.

Chapter 4

—

WINDOWS FORMS

Visual Studio .NET (VS .NET) is an integrated development environment (IDE). While VS .NET has many features, one of the most immediately useful to the J# programmer is its ability to generate code for Windows applications based on a graphical user interface (GUI) that the user designs. In short, you can create your GUI in the Windows Form Designer (WFD), a component of VS .NET that allows you to "paint" your application in a design window. Basically, you drag and drop various elements from a toolbox, and VS .NET generates code to represent these elements and the actions that can be performed on them (such as clicking). The generated code takes the form of event handler methods, which execute when a control that you have added to your interface is activated by a user action (e.g., the user clicks on it).

All of the controls used in the WFD are actually instances of classes found in the System.Windows.Forms namespace. The first topic in this chapter will discuss how controls are represented by classes. The second topic will take a closer look at the properties of some of the most commonly used controls, such as buttons, textboxes, and labels. The last topic of this chapter examines a technology called GDI+, a powerful graphics package that can be used for drawing shapes, filling surfaces with gradients and textures, and loading and manipulating images. GDI+ allows you to add impressive graphical elements to your J# applications with relative ease.

Simple Application

Let's begin with a simple application that will show you just how easy it is to create applications with attractive GUIs using Visual Studio .NET and J#.

Open Visual Studio .NET and click on the **New Project** button to start a new project. Choose the J# Windows Application template, and give your project a name. We'll call ours JSHelloWorld. When the JSHelloWorld solution has been set up, you will be presented with an initial form to which you can add controls, as shown in Figure 4.1.

Open the toolbox on the left side of the window, and drag three controls onto your form: a Label, a TextBox, and a Button. You can place these wherever you like on your form, as illustrated in Figure 4.2. You can change the size and dimensions of a form or control by clicking on it (also known as *highlighting* or *selecting* a control) and dragging any of the eight white bounding squares vertically, horizontally, or diagonally.

Our GUI is fairly useless as it is—the user won't have any idea what each of the controls is for. We can solve this problem by changing the Text property of each of the components. To change a property, high-

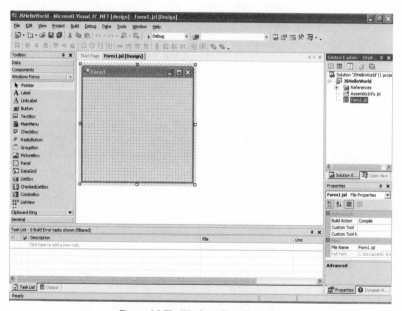

Figure 4.1 The Windows Form Designer

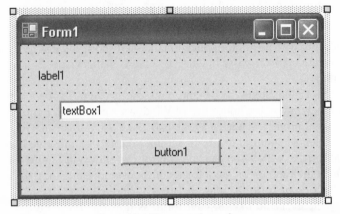

Figure 4.2 Adding controls to a form

light a component (by clicking on it) and then look at the Properties browser located in the bottom right corner of Visual Studio (we introduced the Properties pane in the section called "What Is Visual Studio .NET" in Chapter 1). This box will contain every property that is available to the current control, as well as the value each property is currently set to. Scroll down the list until you find the Text property—this controls the text that appears on the controls themselves. Change the Text property of each component so that your form looks like Figure 4.3.

We could run our application at this point, and it would work fine: we could type text in the textbox and click the **Submit** button. However, at this point, none of the components actually *do* anything. We need to add some code to our application in order to have it actually do something.

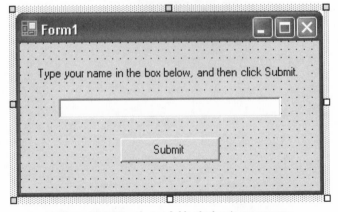

Figure 4.3 Editing the text fields of a form's components

In the case of our application, we want to display a message box (Figure 4.4) with the user's name in it whenever the **Submit** button is clicked.

Double-click on the **Submit** button in the Design window. This will open the code view of your application. Since this is the first time you have double-clicked on this particular control, Visual Studio .NET will also generate a new method that will be called whenever the **Submit** button is clicked. This method is called a handler; we'll look at handlers much more closely in the "Core Concepts" section of this chapter. Now that you are in the code view, you can switch back to the design view at any time by clicking on the **Design** tab, or pressing **Alt-Tab** to cycle through the open windows. For now, stay with the code view.

Inside the button1_Click () method, we need to add a single line of code that will pop up the message we want to display. Listing 4.1 shows that line of code in bold. Note that the MessageBox.Show () method can be used to pop up a simple window with a text message in it (the message should be provided as a parameter to the Show () method).

```
private void button1_Click (Object sender, System.EventArgs e)
{
    MessageBox.Show("Hello, " + textBox1.get_Text() + "!");
}
```

Listing 4.1 Adding code to the Submit button

Note that the button1_click() handler naming scheme demonstrated in Listing 4.1 (control name, underscore, event name) is a convention, not a rule. Although VS .NET will automatically generate handler method names using this naming scheme, you can actually call your event handlers anything you want, as we will see in the "Core Concepts" section.

Our application is complete. Compile and run it by pressing **CTRL + F5,** and you should be presented with the form you just created. Type your name in the textbox, click the **Submit** button, and a message box resembling Figure 4.4 should appear.

Figure 4.4 The message resulting from our Hello World application

You can change the name in the textbox and click the **Submit** button as many times as you want; the application will display a new message box each time. To close the application, simply click on the "X" in the top right corner of the form.

CORE CONCEPTS

Events

Almost any time you interact with an object in a J# Windows application, an event is raised. An *event* is like a message or a signal indicating that something has happened. For example, when you click a button on a Windows Form, the Common Language Runtime raises a Click event. The same thing happens when you click on a label or an image (in a PictureBox control).

Your Windows application is actually sitting in a process loop, waiting for events. Events are queued up and transferred to your handler code automatically. This paradigm is known as an *event-driven* program, and it forms the heart of all graphical user interface design.

Most VS .NET controls have many events associated with them; in addition to Click, a control might support events such as DoubleClick, MouseHover (the mouse stays on top of the control without moving), and Move (the control is moved on the page). For the most part, the following types of actions trigger an event:

- A mouse button is clicked (one or more times) on a control.
- A keyboard action is taken (such as pressing or releasing a key over a textbox).
- The mouse cursor is moved over or off of a control.
- A control is dragged, moved, resized, or otherwise interacted with using the mouse.
- A control leaves or gains focus. A window or a control has *focus* when it is currently active on the screen (i.e., you have clicked on it, or are typing in it, or it is in front of all the other objects).
- A property of the control (color, font, text content, etc.) is changed programmatically.
- Another event or program action triggers an event. For example, timer controls have an event triggered whenever the timer reaches its preset limit.

Not all of these circumstances will apply to every control, and there may be other actions that trigger events, but the preceding list is a good general guide of the events you will be most interested in—at least while you are in the beginning stages of learning J#.

You can see a list of available events for any control by highlighting the control in the Design window and then clicking on the 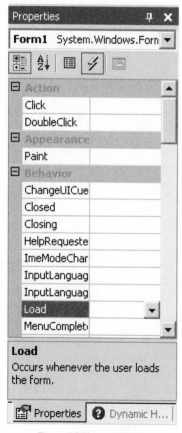 (lightning bolt) icon, which is located at the top of the Properties browser. Scrolling down this list (Figure 4.5) allows you to see all the available events for the current control; it also, as we will see later, allows you to assign special methods called *handlers* to triggered events.

Handlers

A handler is a method that is associated with a specific event. When this event fires, the handler is invoked. When the handler is invoked, any code that you write in the function body of the handler will

Figure 4.5 The event listing

execute. You are, in essence, writing code you wish to execute in response to a particular event. When we added a button to our form in the simple application at the beginning of this chapter and then double-clicked on it, VS .NET automatically created a handler method for us, called `button1_Click()`. Not all handlers are automatically created (and named). However, every control will have at least one default handler that is automatically generated for you if you double-click on the control in the Design window. You can also manually create your own handler methods and assign them to handle one or more events. If you're interested in learning how to manually create event handlers, please see CN JS040001.

When writing code, you will rarely call handlers directly. Handlers are called by the CLR whenever an event fires. You will recall that in our simple application, we never wrote code to explicitly call `button1_Click()`. Instead, the CLR knows that the `Click` event on `Button1` maps to the handler `button1_Click()`. Whenever the `Click` event occurs, the CLR automatically calls all of the delegates for the event, namely `button1_Click()`. In the simple application, there is no other way to activate `button1_Click()`.

The sequence of events that triggers a handler is as follows:

1. The user clicks on a control, such as `button1`. This fires a `Click` event.
2. The CLR checks to see whether any handlers are registered to the `Click` event.
3. The CLR calls `button1_Click()`, a registered handler for `button1`'s `Click` event, and the code inside `button1_Click()` executes.

What you really need to know about this process is that every time an event is fired, a handler may catch the event and activate some code. However, it is worthwhile to look a little deeper into what exactly happens behind the scenes when you assign a handler to an event.

Callbacks and Delegates

A *callback* is frequently defined as an asynchronous notification scheme. We can understand the concept of callbacks best by using a real-life example. Think of a callback as, literally, a "call back." So, for example, if you call a friend on the telephone and she is not there, you don't wait; instead, you leave your name and telephone number on her answering machine. When your friend gets home, she can notify you of her arrival by giving you a call back.

As illustrated in Figure 4.6, callbacks in .NET facilitate this behavior.

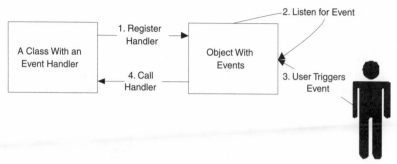

Figure 4.6 Callback behavior in .NET

1. Our class, which contains code for an event handler, *registers* this code with an object that handles events. This step is equivalent to calling your friend's answering machine (event-handling object) and leaving your phone number (the address for your callback function).
2. The object listens for any new events—your friend's answering machine waits patiently until your friend gets home.
3. An event occurs—your friend gets home and plays the message.
4. Your event handler gets called—your friend calls your phone number.

During this process, your program is free to perform other actions, much as you are free to wander around until your friend calls back.

.NET applications use objects called *delegates* to control callback functionality. A delegate is a reference to a particular method, called a *handler method.* Each possible event in your application has its own *delegate chain* (a collection of one or more delegates) that will execute when the event is triggered. When you create and double-click on a Button control in the Design window, for example, Visual Studio creates a handler method (e.g., button1_Click()) and adds the address of that method to the delegate chain for the Click event on Button1.

Because events have chains of delegates and not just one delegate, a single event can have multiple handlers associated with it, which will execute in the order they were added to the delegate chain. (Incidentally, a handler method can also handle more than one event; a reference to the same method is simply added to several events' delegate chains).

Visual Inheritance

Your understanding of class inheritance from Chapter 3 will also allow you to investigate a completely new feature in the .NET Framework called Visual Inheritance. Visual Inheritance is a technique that allows you to apply object inheritance principles to the GUI elements of your application. You can, for example, design a *base* form and then inherit its properties across multiple *derived* forms. As with standard class inheritance, changes to the base form automatically propagate to the derived ones. For more details on class inheritance, see ⟨CN⟩ JS040004.

Topic: The Windows Form Designer

The Windows Form Designer (WFD) allows you to visually, rather than conceptually, create applications in a WYSIWYG (What You See Is What You Get)–style environment. Creating applications using the WFD is simple—you draw your application's graphical elements on a form and then write the event handlers behind them. When you draw a button, change its caption, and then change its size, the WFD translates your manipulations into J# code that represents the button as a Windows Forms class with properties defining the button's size, caption text, and so on.

As the upcoming example will illustrate, code generated by the WFD is placed into a special section of code called a *region,* which is marked with #region and #endregion tags. A region allows a developer to block a section of code together; Visual Studio will place special expand/collapse icons next to regions of code and will allow you to show and hide the regions at will. Most of the time, automatically generated code is placed in a hidden region so that the developer does not have to see or worry about it.

CONCEPTS

Windows Forms Classes

The Windows Forms Classes can be found in the System.Windows.Forms namespace (the J# Windows Application template you select to start a new project automatically puts in a reference to the System.Windows.Forms namespace as a convenience for you). The most important class in System.Windows.Forms is the Control class. Any component in the .NET Framework that has a GUI element must derive from Control, which handles user input and operating system notifications such as repaint requests. The Control class is at the top of the Windows Forms hierarchy that is depicted in Figure 4.7.

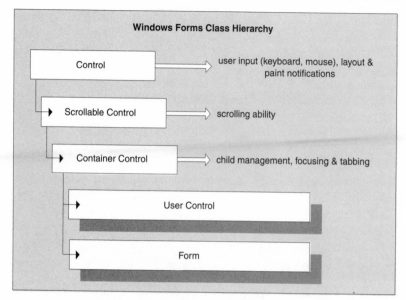

Figure 4.7 The Windows Forms Class Hierarchy

As shown in Figure 4.7, other controls in the Windows Forms framework extend the basic functionality of the Control class. Scrollable-Control adds scrolling ability to a control, while ContainerControl gives a control the ability to house other controls by providing focusing and tabbing functionality. Two descendents of the Control class, User-Control and Form, are the ones you will interact with most often. The Form class is used to create Windows screens and dialog boxes in J#, whereas the UserControl class can be used to create your own custom controls.

Windows Forms Example

In this example we are going to create a simple application using the Windows Form Designer. Begin by creating a J# Windows Application project in VS .NET. After creating your project, VS .NET will bring up the design environment that we first saw in Chapter 1, as shown in Figure 4.8.

Drag a button from the toolbox onto your form, and resize it so that you have something like the screen shown in Figure 4.9.

Double-click button1 and insert the line this.Close(); so that you see the code shown in Figure 4.10.

You have just written your first application using the WFD. You can run the program by pressing **F5** or going to the Debug menu and click-

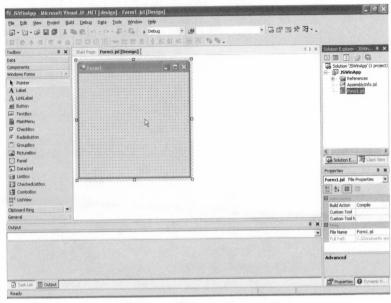

Figure 4.8 VS .NET design environment

ing **Start.** Let's take a close look at the code in Figure 4.10. Notice the following:

- We use the `this` object to represent the current object, which in this case is `Form1`. `this.Close()` closes the form (and stops the application).
- The `button1_Click()` method is associated with the event that occurs when `button1` is clicked. The `button1_Click()` method is referred to as an *event handler.* The method takes `System.Object` and `System.EventArgs` arguments, which will be explained subsequently.
- All of the code is contained in a class called `Form1`, which inherits from the `Windows.Forms.Form` class.
- There is a curious boxed and grayed-out section called "Windows Form Designer generated code." You will rarely need to look at or modify this code, as it performs critical initialization functions for the form. However, we'll peek into the generated code a little later on.

Before we investigate exactly what the WFD is doing, let's take a look at the concepts behind event handlers in Visual Studio .NET (the second point in the preceding list).

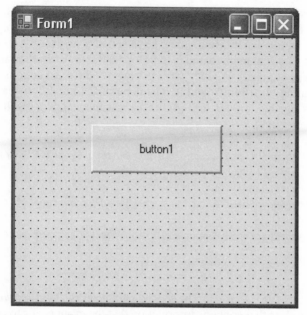

Figure 4.9 A J# application using the WFD

WFD Generated Event Handlers

All event handlers generated by the Windows Form Designer accept the following two parameters:

- Object sender   This parameter represents the entity that invoked the event. Remember from Chapter 3 that everything in J# (and all .NET languages) derives from the Object type. Since anything could conceivably trigger an event, it makes

```
Windows Form Designer generated code

/**
 * The main entry point for the application.
 */
/** @attribute System.STAThread() */
public static void main(String[] args)
{
    Application.Run(new Form1());
}

private void button1_Click (Object sender, System.EventArgs e)
{
    this.Close();
}
```

Figure 4.10 J# application code

sense to use a generic Object to represent it. In Figure 4.10, the entity that raises the button1_Click method would probably be the button itself. Remember however, that button1_Click is just a normal method and is therefore callable from other methods in our class. We may want to perform different actions, depending on who invoked it. The code in Listing 4.2 displays a message box only if button1_Click was invoked as a result of a button click.

```
private void button1_Click (Object sender, System.EventArgs e)
{
  if (sender.equals(button1))
    MessageBox.Show("Event was triggered by button1.") ;
  else
    MessageBox.Show("Event was triggered by someone else!") ;
}
```

Listing 4.2 Differentiating handler actions by sender

- System.EventArgs e The second parameter is a System.Event-Args class that contains information that the event needs to communicate. In practice, event handlers that need to communicate information pass a class that *derives* from System.EventArgs. Because the Click event is very straightforward, it uses a generic EventArgs class.

Back to the WFD

When we started our project, VS .NET automatically created an empty form for us called Form1. Behind the scenes, the WFD created a class in our project called Form1 that inherits from the Form class in the System.Windows.Form namespace. Remember that by inheriting from a class we automatically inherit any methods exposed by that class. Thus, Form1 inherits methods such as Close(), Show(), and Refresh(). It also inherits properties such as Size and Width, which define the dimensions of the form.

The role of the WFD isn't finished. When we added a button to the form, the WFD gave the Form1 class a private variable called button1, which is an instance of the System.Windows.Forms.Button class. The existence of the generated button1 variable may not seem obvious from looking at the code in Figure 4.10, but you can see it if you expand the Windows Form Designer generated code section as shown in Figure 4.11.

If you expand the WFD section, as shown in Figure 4.11, you will see

```
Windows Form Designer generated code

#region Windows Form Designer generated code
/**
 * Required method for Designer support - do not modify
 * the contents of this method with the code editor.
 */
private void InitializeComponent()
{
    this.button1 = new System.Windows.Forms.Button();
```

Figure 4.11 The WFD generated code

that WFD generated code is enclosed within #region and #endregion
tags. Scanning through this code (there is a lot of it), you will see the line
of code shown in Listing 4.3.

```
this.button1 = new System.Windows.Forms.Button() ;
```

Listing 4.3 Creating a button instance inside the WFD generated region

The button1 object itself is actually declared right at the beginning of
the Form1 class (outside the WFD generated region, even though it is actually generated by the WFD) using the line shown in Listing 4.4.

```
private System.Windows.Forms.Button button1 ;
```

Listing 4.4 Declaring the button

This second line (Listing 4.4) declares the button class, while the first
line (Listing 4.3) instantiates it. Look closely, and you will see that the
first line is contained in a private method called InitializeCompo-
nent(). This method is called from the form's constructor method
(Form1(), shown in Listing 4.5), which is called before the form loads.

```
public Form1()
{
  //
  // Required for Windows Form Designer support
  //
  InitializeComponent() ;

  //
  // TODO: Add any constructor code after InitializeComponent
  // call
```

```
        //
}
```

Listing 4.5 Calling InitializeComponent

The InitializeComponent() method instantiates and configures all of the form's contained classes (buttons, labels, pictures, etc.). For example, if you look at the code for InitializeComponent(), you will see the lines shown in Listing 4.6, which determine the button's size and location.

```
this.button1.set_Location(new System.Drawing.Point(80, 88)) ;
this.button1.set_Size(new System.Drawing.Size(136, 48)) ;
```

Listing 4.6 Hidden code for setting graphical properties

These lines were generated by the WFD when you placed the button on the form. If you were to return to the form and resize the button, the WFD would change the second line of code to match your actions. Notice that a control's location and size are specified using the Location and Size properties, which are set in J# using the set_Location() and set_Size() accessor methods, respectively.

You may be wondering whether we can do the reverse. That is, can we change the underlying code and see a corresponding change in the button's size in the design environment? You can, but it is not advisable. The WFD doesn't expect you to modify the code it generates. If you make a change it doesn't understand (e.g., if you delete certain class declarations), it could damage your entire project file. For demonstration purposes, however, let's do something innocuous and change the first parameter in the button's Size property from 100 to 200. Return to the design environment, and the button's width will have increased.

Look (but don't touch!) through the rest of WFD generated code and you will begin to understand the intricacies of the Windows Forms classes. Examine the Form1 class, and you will note that it doesn't contain a Close() method. The absence of Close() may seem odd, given that we used this method in Figure 4.10 to close the form and terminate our application. Again, remember from Chapter 3 that by inheriting from the System's Form class, we automatically inherit its members, including the Close() method. Therefore, our particular form doesn't need its own Close() method unless we want to do something special besides simply closing the form.

Also remember from Chapter 3 that we can override a base class's methods simply by defining a method with the same name and parameters in the subclass. If, for example, we wanted to write our own Refresh() method for Form1, we would do so as shown in Listing 4.7.

```
public void Refresh()
{
  // Do our refresh (perhaps repaint some figures, etc.)

  // Make sure we call Refresh() on Form :
  super.Refresh() ;
}
```

Listing 4.7 Overriding a method

Listing 4.7 illustrates a very important rule when overriding methods of the Windows Form's classes: *be sure to call the base class method you have overridden!* In the preceding code we replaced Form's Refresh() method with our own implementation. However, the Form class from which we inherited also has its own Refresh() code. It is extremely important, therefore, that we call Form's Refresh() method from within our own implementation using J#'s super keyword. As its name suggests, the super keyword can be used to invoke the methods of a superclass from a subclass. If you do not call the parent class method, you may not execute some critical functionality. In the case of Refresh(), for example, you will skip the code that repaints the controls on the page.

Experiment with some other controls in the VS .NET IDE (some of the more common ones are discussed in the next topic), and you will see that developing applications using Windows Forms is extremely easy and user friendly. The primary thing to remember is that—behind the scenes—the WFD converts your controls and their actions into corresponding calls to the Windows Forms classes. The biggest change for Java developers will be getting used to the fact that VS .NET does most of the work for you.

HOW AND WHY

Can I Use the Windows Forms Designer with Other Languages?
Remember from Chapter 1 that assemblies contain language-neutral IL code. The classes in the System.Windows.Forms namespace are no exception and are thus callable from any .NET language, including J#, C#, VB.NET, and Managed C++.

To "paint" applications, however, you need a tool such as the Windows Form Designer that translates your graphical manipulations into code that calls the appropriate classes. The Windows Form Designer in VS .NET is designed with an open architecture, allowing third parties to write code that can leverage the drag-and-drop functionality. However, as of this writing, the WFD can generate code only in J#, VB.NET, C#, and Managed C++. Several third parties have developed, or are developing, additional extensions for languages such as COBOL (Fujitsu's net-Cobol for VS .NET); however, other languages such as C++ and JScript cannot directly use the WFD. If you wish to call the Windows Forms classes using languages not supported by the WFD, you must do so programmatically, without the benefit of an intuitive design environment.

BUGS AND CAVEATS

A Note on Control Names and Event Handler Method Names

If you change the name of your control, don't be surprised when the name of your event handler doesn't change. When you first create your handler code, VS .NET will automatically name your handler after the control, but the name is actually arbitrary. If you then change the name of your control, your handler will keep the original name. So what happens if you try to change the name of your handler to match the control? Your code will not work. Why? You also need to go to the properties for the object, click on the ⚡ icon, and change the registered handler for the method to match your new method name. In other words, set the name of your control before you write any handler code, and then leave the control name as it is! For more details, see ᴄᴺJS040002.

DESIGN NOTES

Don't Forget the Form Properties

As you will see in the next topic, each control has an associated set of properties that let you decide how the control looks or functions. Don't forget that forms have properties, too. You can set the title for the form, how it will minimize or maximize, or even whether it should rearrange controls if the form is stretched. When you read through the next topic, feel free to try out some of the form properties and see what effects they have on your forms' characteristics.

SUMMARY

GUI development in J# is made possible by the Visual Studio .NET IDE and the Windows Form Designer. VS .NET allows you to pictorially design your application and then associate event code with its elements. Behind the scenes, the WFD generates J# code that calls the

System.Windows.Forms classes. This code is placed in a special region of your code listing, denoted by the #region and #endregion tags. You can and should ignore generated code, unless you want to look into the behind-the-scenes details.

The Windows Forms classes follow an object-oriented approach. A form with two buttons, for example, is really an inherited Form class with two private Button class variables. The characteristics of a GUI are represented through the properties these classes expose, such as Size and Location. Because they are really just classes, the GUI elements in J# applications are susceptible to classlike features such as inheritance (⚿JS040007).

Topic: Common Controls in Visual Studio .NET Development

At this point, you have had several opportunities to glance inside the Visual Studio .NET toolbox. In the preceding topic, for example, we took a button from the toolbox and placed it on a form to create a very simple application. In this topic, we'll take a closer look at some of the components you will almost certainly need when developing any kind of GUI. Keep in mind that there are far too many controls available for this book to cover them all; the goal is to give you a good idea of how some simple controls work and what standard properties you should expect to find, so you can explore and experiment with the rest of the tools in the toolbox.

CONCEPTS

Using Controls

As you've already seen, any control in the toolbox can be added to a GUI simply by dragging it onto a form. Most controls, once dragged in, can be adjusted in size horizontally, vertically, or diagonally using the control nodes. Some controls allow size adjustment only across certain axes; a ComboBox, for example, can be stretched only horizontally and not vertically. Some controls actually appear in a separate windowpane. These nongraphical controls, such as timers, cannot be resized at all because they have no graphical component.

Any .NET control can have an event handler method associated with it. This even includes controls that don't appear to be clickable in an application, such as ordinary Label and GroupBox controls. Simply double-click on a control, and VS .NET will create a handler method for it and take you to the code view so you can add handler code. Remember, however, that event handlers are not necessarily limited to being Click methods. More complex components will have different methods that handle their special functionality; a CheckBox, for example, has a Checked-Changed handler method, rather than a Click method.

After dragging and dropping a control onto a form, you will most likely want to adjust one or more of its properties. The Properties browser, as explained in Chapter 1, is located, by default, in the bottom right corner of your screen. The available properties will change depending on what control (or form) you have highlighted in the Design window. You can change any property simply by clicking on its value in the Properties browser and then typing or selecting a new value. There are many properties that are available to almost all controls (Name, Text, Font, BackColor, etc.) Most of these are self-explanatory. Other properties, however, are specific to a control; we will explore some of these properties as we look at some common controls in detail.

Accessing Properties from Code

The Properties browser isn't the only way to change a control's properties. Remember that controls are represented by actual classes in code, just like everything else in .NET. This means that they are completely accessible from your application's code using standard set_ and get_ accessor methods. An *accessor method* allows you to either change (set) or retrieve (get) the value of a property. The standard naming convention in J# is for these methods to start with "set_" or "get_" and end with the name of the property. For example, Text1.get_BackColor() would return the background color for the textbox named Text1.

In order to access a control from code, however, you need to know the name of that control. As you add controls to your Windows Form, .NET will automatically assign them nondescriptive names and numbers. For example, if we dragged five labels onto a form, we would end up with five Label objects, named label1, label2, label3, label4, and label5. It is often a good idea to change the names of your controls so they are more indicative of what the control is actually for. For example, the five labels we just added could be renamed MainTitleLabel, SubTitleLabel, DescriptionLabel, and so on. You can change the name of any control you create by editing its Name property in the Properties browser. The control will then be accessible via that name from your form's underlying code.

For example, the code in Listing 4.8 is an event handler for a Button named SubmitButton that changes the text in a Label object named OutputLabel.

```
private void SubmitButton_Click (Object sender,
                                 System.EventArgs e)
{
  OutputLabel.set_Text("All your base are belong to us.") ;
}
```

Listing 4.8 Accessing properties from code

Note that VS .NET will automatically generate handler methods with the correct names for you as long as you change the control's name *before* you create its handler method. As noted in the previous topic's "Bugs and Caveats" section, if you change a control's name and it already has a handler (or handlers) assigned to it, the handler will still work, but its method name will not reflect the actual name of the control. The process of changing control and handler names after creation is somewhat involved—see ⚷JS040002 for details.

Common Controls
The following are some of the more common controls in J# GUIs, with explanations of their essential properties.

Label
A label is the standard means of adding text to a GUI in a J# application. Labels have no moving controls and are not meant to be clicked, edited, or dragged (although you can actually associate a Click event handler with one simply by double-clicking on it). Figure 4.12 shows a simple label. Note that in this topic, we will show controls as they appear when the application is actually running and not as they appear in the Design window.

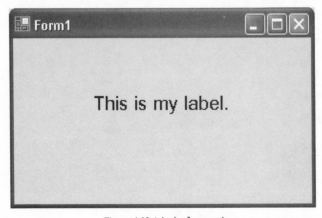

Figure 4.12 A Label *control*

Some of the properties you will often want to change for label controls include the following:

- **Font** This is actually a collection of properties that includes (font) Name, Size, Bold, Italic, and other standard font features. Most of these will be familiar to anyone who has worked with Windows fonts before in applications such as Microsoft Word.
- **Text** This is the text that appears in your label. Text inside labels is automatically multiline and will run off the bottom right corner of the label if there is more text than will fit. You can also adjust the location of your text within the label using the Text-Align property, which defaults to TopLeft for labels.
- **Image** This property allows you to have an image as a label instead of (or in addition to) text. Any text you put in the label will appear superimposed on the image.

Remember that even though you can add a Click handler to a label, that doesn't mean you should. Most users will not be expecting a label to do anything, so if you want to have an effective GUI, try to make clickable objects more apparent (i.e., a button).

Button
Buttons are the primary action controls in most GUIs. Most often, a button will be used to do something with information the user has put into other controls (such as textboxes). As we saw in the previous topic, double-clicking a button control will open its Click method, into which you can add code that will execute when the user clicks the button. Figure 4.13 shows a standard button in action.

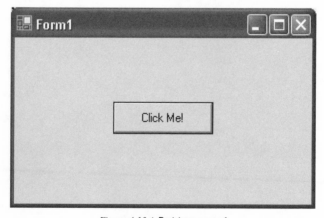

Figure 4.13 A Button *control*

The most common properties for the Button control are the same as those we discussed for the Label control. One difference is that the TextAlign property defaults to MiddleCenter for buttons, instead of TopLeft.

TextBox

The TextBox control is a simple data entry field. Generally, it consists of a white box into which the user can type text. A common paradigm is to have the user type information into a TextBox marked by a Label, and then do something with that information when the user clicks a Button. Figure 4.14 shows a simple TextBox.

Some of the properties you will often want to change for TextBox controls include the following:

- **Text** In the case of a TextBox, the Text property allows you to set the text that *starts* in the field. Because of the nature of the TextBox control, the user can delete, modify, and replace this text once the application is running. If, for some reason, you want a TextBox that cannot be edited, you can set its ReadOnly property to True.
- **MaxLength** This allows you to specify a maximum length for the text in this textbox. By default, the MaxLength value is 32767, which is the largest size allowed for a text string. You might want to reduce this size if you know that the text that will be entered is of a certain length.
- **Multiline** You may have noticed that, by default, a TextBox control can be resized horizontally but not vertically. This is because a TextBox defaults to single-line mode. If you want the user to be able to enter multiple lines of text (and you want words

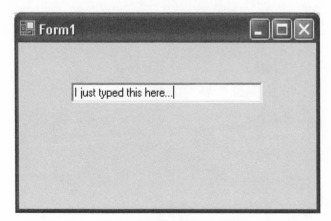

Figure 4.14 A TextBox *control*

to wrap over lines instead of running off the end), you need to change the `Multiline` property to `True`. Once you turn on `Multiline` support, you will also be able to resize your `TextBox` vertically.

- **PasswordChar**   This field allows you to set a character that will be displayed to the user instead of what he or she actually types. For example, if you set `PasswordChar`'s value to * and the user types "hello," he or she will see "*****" instead, even though the application will know that the `TextBox` actually contains "hello." Hiding text is useful if you're creating an application that requires users to type in a password and you don't want prying eyes to be able to see what they are typing.

CheckBox and RadioButton

`CheckBox` and `RadioButton` controls allow you to provide users with sets of options from which they can choose. They differ slightly in behavior, however (beyond the fact that a `CheckBox` uses a check mark and a `RadioButton` uses a dot).

Users can check (or uncheck) as many `CheckBox` controls as they want. This means that if you put multiple `CheckBox` controls on a form, all of them can be checked simultaneously. `RadioButton` controls generally allow only one of a series of options to be selected. If you have three `RadioButtons` in a form, only one can be selected at a time; if the user clicks a different one, it will become selected and the previous choice will be deselected. Basically, `CheckBox` controls ask the user to "choose a bunch of these," and `RadioButton` controls ask the user to "choose one of these." Figure 4.15 shows some `CheckBox` and `RadioButton` controls in action.

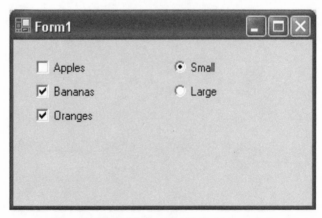

Figure 4.15 `CheckBox` *and* `RadioButton` *controls*

The only property that you'll probably want to change when adding CheckBox and RadioButton controls is the Checked property, which allows you to check certain items by default. With a set of CheckBox controls, it's usually fine to leave all the items unchecked by default. With a RadioBox set, it's recommended that you check at least one of the items to start with. Otherwise, the user might submit the form without selecting any of the options, which could result in bad data for whatever code processes the form.

GroupBox
One question that might have occurred to you when reading the previous section is: How can we have more than one set of RadioButton controls on a single form? We might have two completely separate lists of items, each of which requires that the user choose one, but we don't want selecting an item in one list to clear our selection in the other list.

The solution is to place the lists in separate GroupBox controls. A GroupBox allows you to group other controls together so they will not interfere with one another. It also allows you to organize your GUI in a more constructive manner. To add RadioButtons (or any other item) to a GroupBox, simply create a new GroupBox and then drag the other items into it. Listing 4.12 shows an example in which we have two GroupBox controls with some RadioButton controls inside each. As you can see in Figure 4.16, we have selected one item in each list to show how the two lists are no longer connected.

PictureBox
A PictureBox control allows you to add images to your application. These images can simply be for decorative purposes, or you can add

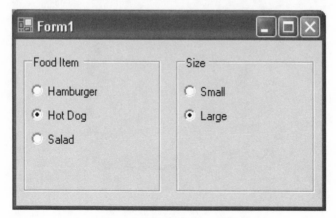

Figure 4.16 **GroupBox** *controls*

handlers to them (just as with any other .NET control). Figure 4.17 shows a PictureBox control in an active form. You select an image to go in the PictureBox using its Image property. Visual Studio will allow you to use a dialog box to select a Bitmap, JPEG, or GIF from a folder on your machine.

Besides Image, the most important property of a PictureBox control is the SizeMode property, which allows you to indicate how the image should react when you adjust the size of the PictureBox in the Design window. The following options are possible:

- Normal   This is the default setting. The picture is placed in the upper left corner of the PictureBox and will be clipped if it is larger than the PictureBox. If the PictureBox is larger than the image, the extra space will be filled with the current BackColor value for the PictureBox.
- StretchImage   The image will grow and stretch as the size of the picture box is changed, always matching it. The image in Figure 4.17 was obtained using StretchImage (which is why it looks squashed).
- AutoSize   The PictureBox is always the size of the picture it contains (i.e., the actual size of the image in the file). When AutoSize mode is set, you cannot adjust the size of the PictureBox.
- CenterImage   The picture is centered in the PictureBox. If it is larger than the PictureBox, it is clipped on all sides. As with Normal, any extra space will be filled by the BackColor.

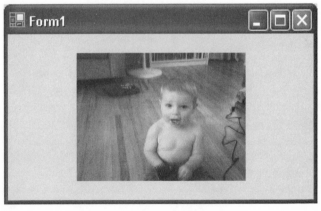

Figure 4.17 A PictureBox control

Timer

A Timer control allows you to have code execute repeatedly on a timed interval. It is quite different from the other controls we have looked at so far, and, indeed, we included it in this chapter simply to demonstrate a control that is used for something other than user data entry.

When you create a Timer object by dragging one from the toolbox, it does not appear on the form as did the other controls in this topic. Instead, it will appear as an icon, floating on its own at the bottom of the Design window. This icon indicates that a Timer object exists in your application, but it will not be visible to the user when the application is run.

If you click on the Timer object and examine its properties, you will see that it actually has very few in comparison to the other controls we have seen. In fact, in order to use the Timer, you really need to know about only two properties.

- Enabled A Boolean property that simply indicates whether the timer is running or not. Enabled is False by default. You can set it to True using the Properties browser, or you can activate it from your code at some time during your application's execution. When the value is true, the Timer will start counting down until the Interval is reached, at which time, the Tick event will be fired. You can also start a timer running for your code using the Timer.Start() method, which is just a shortcut for Timer.set_Enabled(true).
- Interval This is the time, in milliseconds (i.e., thousandths of a second), between ticks on the Timer. Each time the Timer ticks, an event occurs and can be handled by a customized Tick method.

Double-clicking on a Timer control will open its Tick method, into which you can place the code you want to run each time the Timer ticks. For example, the code in Listing 4.9 will add the word "Plink!" to a TextBox each time the Timer's interval runs down.

```
private void timer1_Tick (Object sender, System.EventArgs e)
{
  textBox1.set_Text(textBox1.get_Text() + "Plink! ") ;
}
```

Listing 4.9 Using a Timer *control*

There are many other controls that will appear in this "icon section" at the bottom of the Design window instead of on the form itself, such as ErrorProvider, PrintDocument, or PageSetupDialog. You can find information on these and others in the MSDN Library documentation.

HOW AND WHY

How Can I Add Event Handlers to Controls for Events Other Than the Default?

Every control has a default event and corresponding event handler that will be generated when you double-click on the control in the Design window. For example, both labels and buttons automatically generate Click event handlers.

But suppose we wanted to add a handler for another event that is supported by a control? For example, suppose we wanted to allow users to double-click on a PictureBox to view a larger version of that picture. This is actually quite simple. In the Windows Forms Designer view, highlight the control for which you want to add an event handler and then click on the ⚡ icon that appears at the top of the Properties browser. You will see a list of the events that can be triggered by the selected control. Find the event you want to handle in the list, and then either use the drop-down menu next to it to find an existing method that should handle the event or type the name of a new method in the box. If you do the latter, VS .NET will automatically generate a new empty handler method for you with the name you specified. You can then fill in whatever code you want to execute when the event occurs.

How Can I Change the Properties of a Form?

A form is treated like an object in the Design window, just like all the other controls. To access its properties, you can simply click in any empty space on the form or on its menu bar. Its properties will then be accessible in the Properties browser. You might, for example, want to change the form's Text property so that a title other than "Form1" will appear in its title bar. You can also change its color, dimensions, and behavior.

How Can I Set Up a Tab Order between Controls?

Many users find it faster and easier to fill out forms or use GUIs if they can use the **Tab** key to move between controls, rather than having to click on each one with the mouse. For example, if you had a series of 10 textboxes you needed users to fill out, it would be easier for them to fill one out and press **Tab** to get to the next one rather than reaching for the mouse every time.

Tabbing is automatically supported in any J# GUI you create. However, the order in which the **Tab** button carries users from one control to the next will, by default, depend on the order in which you added the controls to the form. The default order may not be the optimal choice, because you don't want users jumping all over the form, filling out fields in strange sequences. The solution to this problem is to manipulate the TabIndex properties of each control in your form. Each control should be given a TabIndex value from zero (0) to however many controls you have. When the application runs, users will be able to tab from one control to the next, following the TabIndex values in numerical order. Note that some controls, such as Labels, are not meant to be selected and therefore will not allow users to tab to them, even if they have an appropriate TabIndex value.

The easiest way to set the tab order is simply to choose **View → Tab Order** from the main menu. Each control that can be tabbed to will have a small number indicating its current TabIndex. Simply click on the controls to reset these values.

BUGS AND CAVEATS

Page Resizing
One of the classic problems with any GUI is that if users shrink or stretch the form, the various controls should shrink or grow appropriately. Developing code to handle page resizing is traditionally a difficult problem. With Windows Forms, however, you can simply set a few properties on each object to link it to a relative position on the form. Specifically, by setting the Anchor and Dock properties, you can create controls that will automatically move when the form is resized. For details, see ⟋JS040003.

DESIGN NOTES

Stick to Expected Behavior
Most software users expect to be able to look at a GUI and intuitively know what data to enter and which buttons to push. You can help users by always adding labels to your textboxes, setting your tab order from top to bottom and left to right, and building in other normal features. If, on the other hand, you choose to build in nontypical behavior, you can make the program almost unusable.

SUMMARY

The controls in this topic are only the beginning. As you will have noticed by now, there are dozens of controls in the toolbox that we do not have room to cover in a CodeNotes book. Although labels, textboxes, buttons, and graphics will probably cover your bases a lot of the time, as you become more familiar with J# and .NET you will likely find yourself wanting to experiment with additional controls. Most of .NET's controls are self-explanatory, and if you need help, the documentation is always only a few clicks away. As a suggested starting point, take a look at the ListView and TreeView controls. These controls are more complicated than the controls described in this chapter, but they are also used very regularly.

Topic: GDI+

GDI+ is a powerful library that can be used to render graphics in your applications. Using the classes in the System.Drawing namespace, you can draw two-dimensional (2D) graphics, perform image and font manipulation, and carry out sophisticated operations such as texture and gradient filling. GDI+ also includes native support for graphics formats such as JPEG and GIF.

As its name suggests, GDI+ is an evolved version of the Windows Graphics Device Interface (GDI), a subsection of the Windows API used to draw graphics and formatted text on video displays. GDI is a complex tool intended for C/C++ developers and requires you to familiarize yourself with low-level concepts such as device contexts, coordinate spaces, and graphic objects. Because of this, GDI is often spurned in favor of more intuitive frameworks such as the Microsoft Foundation Classes (MFC), OpenGL, and DirectX.

Although GDI is a low-level library, GDI+ is not. The functions exposed through GDI+ are both simple and powerful. As we will see, J# developers can leverage GDI+ functions such as DrawLine() and DrawEllipse() to create complicated graphics with fairly little code. In addition, you can use GDI+ to create GUI windows that are not rectangular and perform other graphics tricks that are available in most languages.

CONCEPTS

GDI Subsections

The GDI+ framework can be broken down into three subsections:

- **2D graphics** These classes, found in the System.Drawing and System.Drawing.Drawing2D namespaces, are used to draw lines, ellipses, and curves and to fill surfaces with textures and gradients. There are also classes for matrix operations (used to transform images) as well as advanced image techniques such as alpha blending, which allows surfaces to behave translucently.

- **Image manipulation** This contains classes that render and crop images in a variety of formats including BMP, GIF, JPEG, EXIF, PNG, and TIFF. It also contains the Metafile class (not to be confused with Metadata) that allows a sequence of drawing routines to be recorded, saved to disk, and played back at a later time. These classes are found in the System.Drawing.Imaging namespace.
- **Typography** This includes classes to render fonts with special effects such as texture and gradient filling. These classes are found in the System.Drawing.Text namespace.

The Graphics Class

GDI+ is centered around the Graphics class, which represents a drawing surface such as a form or PictureBox. You use the Graphics class to perform the majority of operations in GDI+, be it drawing an ellipse or rendering an image. Depending on the operation at hand, the Graphics class is used in conjunction with the following classes.

- **Brush** The Brush class and its descendents (SolidBrush, HatchBrush, LinearGradientBrush) are used to fill a surface with colors, patterns, or even bitmaps. When calling a Graphic object's FillRegion() or FillRectangle() methods, for example, you pass it the brush used to fill the plane.
- **Pen** The Pen class is used when a Graphics object draws lines, curves, and shapes using methods such as DrawLine(), Draw-Curve(), and DrawEllipse(). To draw a circle on a form, for example, we could use the code in Listing 4.10.

```
Graphics myGraphics;
Pen myPen = new Pen(Color.get_Black()) ;
myGraphics = this.CreateGraphics() ;
myGraphics.DrawEllipse(myPen,100,100,50,50) ;
```

Listing 4.10 Drawing a circle on a form

The CreateGraphics() method of a form returns a Graphics object representing the form's surface. Once we have obtained a Graphics object, we use its DrawEllipse() method to draw a circle (geometry review: a circle is really an ellipse whose width and height are the same). The ellipse is drawn with the Pen object we declared—in this case, one that results in an ellipse whose outline is black. It is important to note that when using GDI+, you specify coordinates using pixel values. The second and third parameters of DrawEllipse() specify the center of the ellipse relative to the form, while the fourth and fifth parameters specify the ellipse's height and width, respectively.

• **Font**   Use the Font class to describe the appearance of text you wish to render on the screen. You will most often use Font with a Graphic object's DrawString() method. The concept of "rendering text" may seem odd until you realize that you can give fonts a gradient or textured background. You can also render a font using *antialiasing* techniques, which give it a smooth appearance, or using Microsoft's ClearType font technology, which can improve a font's appearance on LCD screens. For details on GDI+'s font options, see ⟨CN⟩JS040006.

GDI+ EXAMPLE

J# developers rarely have to directly interface with GDI+, as most simple graphics also have wrapper classes in the .NET Framework. One exception is when you want to create a form with irregular dimensions, such as the one depicted in Figure 4.18.

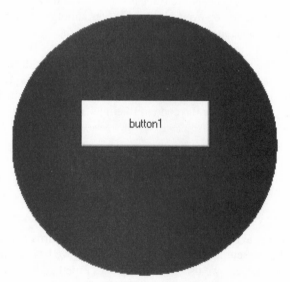

Figure 4.18 An irregular form

You could use an elliptical form like the one in Figure 4.18 in a number of scenarios: for a splash screen, for a tooltip form that appears when a user scrolls over a certain control, and so forth. Creating an irregularly shaped form with GDI+ is straightforward, given the Framework's object-oriented design. For this example, we will give the J# application you created at the beginning of this chapter (Figure 4.9) an elliptical appearance.

Adjusting the Form Properties

To begin, bring up the J# application we developed in Figure 4.9 (if you haven't already done so, refer to the beginning of this chapter to create this project). Use the Property toolbox to change the form's FormBorderStyle to None, which removes its status bar and gives it a floating appearance (Figure 4.19).

Next, add the line in Listing 4.11 to the top of the form's code to reference some of the classes we will be using (note that the VS.IDE will automatically reference the System.Drawing namespace).

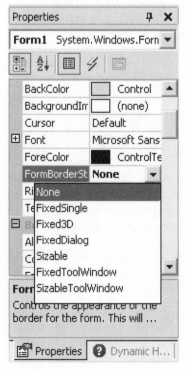

Figure 4.19 Changing the form's border style to None

```
import System.Drawing.Drawing2D.*;
```

Listing 4.11 Referencing the Drawing2D *classes*

Using the GDI+ Classes on the Form

Now add the highlighted code in Listing 4.12 to the form's constructor method (Form1()).

```
public Form1()
{
    //
    // Required for Windows Form Designer support
    //
    InitializeComponent();

    // our GDI+ code to create an elliptical form
    GraphicsPath gPath = new GraphicsPath();
    gPath.AddEllipse(0,0,this.get_ClientSize() .get_Width(),
                        this.get_ClientSize() .get_Height());
    this.set_Region(new Region(gPath));
}
```

Listing 4.12 GDI+ code to produce an irregular form

Remember that the form's constructor is called before the form has loaded. Also note that whenever code is added to the Form1() method, *you must place it after the call to* InitializeComponent(). As we discovered at the beginning of this chapter, the InitializeComponent() method is generated by the WFD to initialize the form (i.e., to configure the form itself and to instantiate the controls it contains, such as buttons and labels). Performing operations on a form before it has been properly initialized can have disastrous consequences (trying to resize a form's button, for example, before InitializeComponent() instantiated it would result in a NullReference exception).

The code we have added gives our form an elliptical appearance. To understand how it does this, we must define some GDI+ terminology:

- **Path** Think of a path as a surface where lines and figures can be drawn. Either the path can be virtual, meaning it has no representation on screen, or it can represent a tangible surface that exists on a form, PictureBox, or any other GUI control.
- **Region** A region specifies the permissible drawing area of a window.

The first two lines of our code declare a virtual path using the Graph-icsPath object. The third line adds an ellipse to the path, whose height and width match that of the form. Remember that an ellipse isn't actually drawn on the screen—the path and its contents are an abstract representation in the computer's memory.

The final line does all the work. One of the properties of the Control class (remember from Figure 4.7 that the Form class ultimately inherits from the Control class) is Region, which specifies the viewable region of the control. The final line sets the viewable region of the form to the region defined by our virtual path, which consists of the single ellipse. The result is a form much like the one in Figure 4.18.

Further GDI+ Enhancements

To demonstrate some additional features of GDI+, we'll give the form a gradient background. We do this by adding the method in Listing 4.13 to the Form1 class.

```
protected void OnPaint(PaintEventArgs e)
{
    LinearGradientBrush myBrush = new LinearGradientBrush(
                            new Point (0,0),
                            new Point(300,300),
                            Color.get_Black(),
                            Color.get_White());
    e.get_Graphics() .FillRegion(myBrush, this.get_Region());
}
```

Listing 4.13 Giving an irregular form a gradient background

The Form class's OnPaint routine, which we override in Listing 4.13, is called whenever the form is painted on the screen. OnPaint supplies us with a PaintEventArgs class, which provides (among other things) the form's Graphics object, representing the form's surface. Using this Graphics object, we can modify the form's surface as we please (draw a line, draw an ellipse, etc.). In our case, we want to fill its background. To do so, we a need a brush object—in this case, a LinearGradientBrush. We could also have used a SolidBrush or TextureBrush to fill the form with a solid color or texture, respectively.

Run the application again, and the form should appear as in Figure 4.20.

We specified that the gradient should fade from black to white in the third and fourth arguments of the LinearGradient declaration. The first two arguments specify the coordinates at which the gradient begins and ends. Try playing around with different start and stop points, as well as

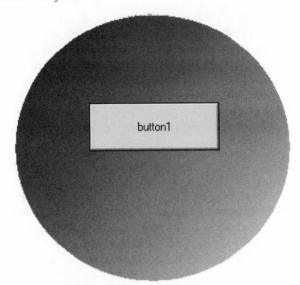

Figure 4.20 An irregular and gradient-filled form

different gradient colors, using the `Colors` enumerations (`Color.Blue`, `Color.Red`, etc.).

This example is but a survey of the numerous features in the GDI+ Framework—one which you are highly encouraged to explore. With its support for 2D graphics, typography, and image manipulation, colorful, attention-grabbing GUIs are easy to create and modify.

HOW AND WHY

How Do I Shade Fonts?
As mentioned earlier in this topic, GDI+ also gives you great control over rendering text on the screen. For example, using the `Font` controls, the right `Brush`, and the `Graphics.DrawString()` method, you can create text that has a drop shadow and shades in color. For an example and details on fonts and GDI+, see JS040006.

BUGS AND CAVEATS

Irregular Forms Can Clip Controls
The code in Listing 4.11 creates the irregular form at runtime. That means that during your design phase, you are still looking at a rectangu-

lar form. You have to be careful how you place your controls, or they may get clipped by the GDI+ commands. Unfortunately, you can't see where the path is going to be until you run your program, so some testing is required when you work with irregular forms. Also, some properties, such as the form title, may get clipped. In the preceding example, the form title is in the upper left-hand corner, so it's no longer visible once the GDI+ code is applied to make the circular form.

DESIGN NOTES

Isolate Your Graphics
As mentioned earlier, GDI+ generally works on units of pixels. If you are creating specialized graphics, you should apply them inside a Picture-Box, where you have better control over the size and shape. If you work directly in the form, you may find your graphics slipping under other controls or becoming oddly shaped when the form is resized.

SUMMARY

GDI+ is an evolution of the Graphic Device Interface (GDI) for the managed environment that allows you to draw 2D graphics and perform image and font manipulation. At the heart of GDI+ is the Graphics class that represents a drawing surface. The Graphics class is used in conjunction with the Brush, Pen, and Font classes to fill surfaces, draw shapes, and render text, respectively. In addition to these basic operations, GDI+ offers several advanced imaging techniques such as gradient and texture surface filling, antialiasing, and matrix operations.

Chapter Summary

Desktop applications in J# are designed using Windows Forms, a set of classes in the System.Windows.Forms namespace. Using the Windows Forms classes is a transparent process thanks to the Windows Form Designer (WFD), which allows you to create applications in a WYSIWYG environment. You "paint" your applications in the Design window, and the WFD produces J# code behind the scenes to correspond to your actions.

GUIs that are designed with Windows Forms can be visually inherited. Inheriting a GUI inherits not only its physical characteristics but its underlying code as well. Visual Inheritance adheres to the rules of object inheritance as discuss in Chapter 3—if a base form's control is marked `Private`, then it cannot be modified in the inherited form, whereas if it is marked `Public`, then it can be modified.

Chapter 5

—

ASP.NET

ASP stands for Active Server Pages. The original version of ASP was a Microsoft framework and scripting language that could be intermeshed with HTML documents to create Web pages with dynamic content in response to user actions. ASP allowed you to insert blocks of VBScript or JScript code into special elements on an HTML-like page. ASP pages were processed on the back end and the special elements were rendered into standard HTML, which was then sent to the user to be displayed in a browser.

ASP.NET is Microsoft's new version of ASP for the .NET Framework. Unlike its predecessor, ASP.NET allows you to write Web Applications using any .NET language such as VB.NET, C#, or J#. While all of these languages can be inserted in special blocks on your ASP.NET pages, or in linked CodeBehind files, there is a better way: with ASP.NET, you can design Web Application GUIs using the drag-and-drop form design approach that made Visual Studio popular. As we will see throughout this chapter, designing these Web Forms is just as easy as designing the standard Windows Forms discussed in Chapter 4.

ASP.NET is a server-side technology that requires the installation of Microsoft Internet Information Services (IIS). Before running any of the examples in this chapter, you need to have IIS installed on your machine, as detailed in Chapter 2.

ASP.NET offers some very valuable features, including the following:

- *Intuitive GUI design.* With ASP.NET you can design Web Applications as you do in a normal Windows application, by dragging and dropping GUI elements in a sophisticated design environment.
- *Support for compiled languages.* In addition to supporting the traditional set of scripting languages, ASP.NET also supports fully compiled languages such as J# and VB.NET. This means that instead of using VBScript or JScript, a developer can use J# and access that language's features, such as strong typing and object-oriented programming.
- *Greater support for different browsers via server-side controls and events.* Following object-oriented design principles, ASP.NET pages make use of server-side controls called ASP.NET Web Controls. These controls are instantiated on the server and, like regular objects, have associated methods, properties, and events. The advantage of server-side controls is that they render themselves as standard HTML code that differentiates depending on the capabilities of the client browser. In other words, an advanced browser will automatically receive advanced features, while an older browser will still receive readable HTML. Since the controls reside completely on the server and only HTML is returned to the client, browsers can be completely unaware of the Common Language Runtime. Thus, virtually any browser can access an ASP.NET page.
- *Separation of code from content.* ASP.NET allows the developer to separate script code from HTML by placing the code in a separate .jsl file and then linking to that file from the HTML page. This allows for a clean separation of code from content and formatting, and promotes code reuse. Remember, however, that the advantage of ASP.NET is that you really don't have to think about HTML at all—you simply code as though you were working with Windows Forms.

As you will see throughout this chapter, almost every new feature introduced by ASP.NET is designed to provide tremendous improvements for rapid Web Application development. The advanced GUI design, language-format separation, encapsulation of HTML, and masking of client-side/server-side issues makes ASP.NET a very powerful choice for designing Web pages.

As an alternative to Visual Studio .NET and IIS for Web development, however, you might want to explore Web Matrix. Web Matrix is a free, community-supported ASP.NET development tool by Microsoft that includes a built-in lightweight Web server (see 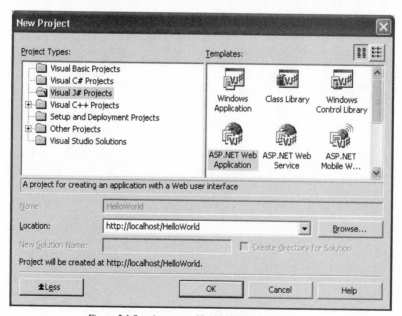CN⟩JS050002 for more details).

Simple Application

Creating a simple ASP.NET application is actually very similar to creating the simple Windows Form application from Chapter 4. Start by opening Visual Studio .NET 2003 and clicking on the **New Project** button. This will open the New Project window. Select **Visual J# Projects** from the **Project Types** box, and choose **ASP.NET Web Application** from the **Templates** box, as shown in Figure 5.1.

Choose a name for your application by changing the text in the **Location** box. Note that you should generally leave the beginning of the URL as http://localhost/ for the examples in this book. This indicates that the Web Application will be running on your local machine, and you will be able to access it there from your Web browser. The text after http://localhost/ can be anything you like; for our sample application, we will use HelloWorld.

Once you've named your application, click the **OK** button to con-

Figure 5.1 Starting a new J# ASP.NET Web Application

tinue. Visual Studio will then set up your new Web Application. This setup includes creating a *virtual root* in Internet Information Services, which allows IIS to host your application at the location you specified. Visual Studio will also produce a good deal of pregenerated J# and ASP.NET code for you, so you can see some results right away.

Adding Controls

As you can see from Figure 5.2, ASP.NET applications start in the design view. From this view, you can construct your page by dragging and dropping components from the toolbox (a) on the left side of the screen, and then configuring those components in the Properties box (b).

Expand the toolbox, and you will see that a new section of controls is available under the heading Web Forms, as shown in Figure 5.3. These are Web Controls, and they can be dragged and dropped onto ASP.NET pages in order to add interactivity to them. You will notice that most standard Windows controls have similar Web Controls that mirror the same functionality in an online environment. What happens behind the scenes is, as we'll see, entirely different.

We'll create a simple application by dragging and dropping a Button, a TextBox, and two Labels onto the WebForm, as shown in Figure 5.4. You can change the text of the labels and button by editing their Text properties in the Properties manager. For our example, we changed the following:

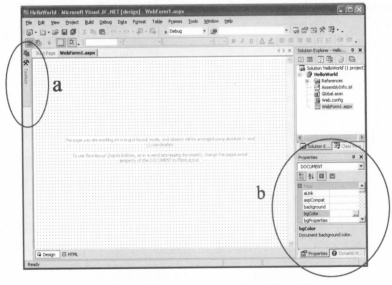

Figure 5.2 Default design view of a J# ASP.NET application

- Label1.Text to "Type your name here:"
- Label2.Text to blank (i.e., we removed the value of the Text property entirely)
- Button1.Text to "Submit"

This application will allow a user to type his or her name in the provided textbox and then click the **Submit** button to display a welcome

Figure 5.3 Web Controls in the VS .NET toolbox

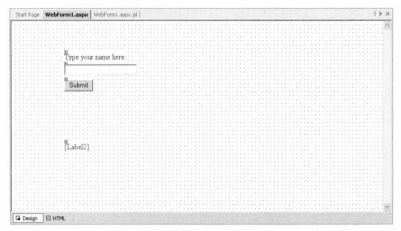

Figure 5.4 HelloWorld *Web Form*

message. The custom welcome message will appear in Label2. In order to do this, however, we need to add a line of code to the CodeBehind file for the Submit button. The CodeBehind file is just like the code view from the Windows Forms discussed in Chapter 4; that is, this file can capture events created by user actions, such as clicking on a button. We'll look more closely at the CodeBehind file in general in the first topic of this chapter. For now, we will examine the CodeBehind file specifically for our HelloWorld application.

The CodeBehind File

You can access any Web Control's CodeBehind by double-clicking on it in the design view. Double-click on the **Submit** button to access its Code-Behind file. Visual Studio .NET will open a file called WebForm1.aspx.jsl, which represents the pure J# code that initializes and controls the Web Form. Each Web Form has its own CodeBehind file.

If you examine WebForm1.aspx.jsl, you should find a method that looks like Listing 5.1.

```
private void Button1_Click (Object sender, System.EventArgs e)
{}
```

Listing 5.1 The Button1 *handler*

As you might recall from Chapter 4, this method is called a handler. This particular handler handles the event triggered when the user clicks the Button1 control. We're going to add a line of code to this handler that will make a message appear in Label2 when the **Submit** button is clicked. This line of code is shown in Listing 5.2.

```
Label2.set_Text("Hello, " + TextBox1.get_Text() + "!");
```

Listing 5.2 J# code for the HelloWorld application

As you can see from Listing 5.2, you can get and set the values of Web Control properties using set_ and get_ accessor methods, just as you can with Windows control properties. This line of code sets the Text value of Label2 to "Hello," plus the name that the user entered into the textbox. It's also the only line of code we need for this application to work as planned.

Running the Application
Press **CTRL + F5** to compile and run the HelloWorld Web Application. Visual Studio will automatically open an instance of Internet Explorer to the correct URL, so you can test it right away. Try entering a name in the textbox and clicking the **Submit** button; the results should resemble Figure 5.5.

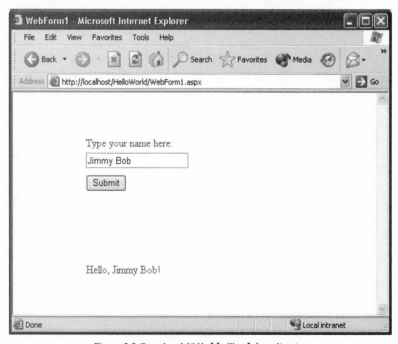

Figure 5.5 Completed J# HelloWorld application

You can find complete source code for this simple application at o**CN**JS050003.

CORE CONCEPTS

HTTP

The Hypertext Transfer Protocol (HTTP) is the communications protocol for the Internet. When you access a Web page, the information is transferred from your client (a Web browser like Internet Explorer) to the server (the website) and back again using HTTP. This ubiquitous protocol is a standard defined by the World Wide Web Consortium (W3C).

HTTP is a *stateless* protocol, which means that each time you access a website, the call is anonymous. Neither the client nor the server keeps track of previous HTTP calls. You can, therefore, think of HTTP calls as "self-destructing" messages that disappear as soon as the receiver has the information. To allow for a level of continuity in your applications (i.e., to maintain the client's identification as he or she browses through multiple pages), you must use state-related technologies such as cookies and Session objects, which we will discuss briefly in this chapter.

Web Server

In order for a computer to *host* Web Applications, it must contain a Web server. A Web server is a software entity that listens for incoming HTTP requests from other computers, processes them appropriately, and sends back HTTP responses to the requesting machines. On Microsoft Windows Server products (NT 4, 2000, and XP), this Web server is called Internet Information Services (IIS). Windows client products (95, 98, and Millennium) contain a less capable Web server called Personal Web Server. Some examples of non-Microsoft Web servers are Apache, iPlanet, Lotus Domino, and Orion.

Most Web servers can be extended with plug-in modules often called *engines* or *runtimes*. The basic Web server can handle ordinary HTML and images, but is often not designed to handle server-side code such as ASP.NET. The runtime plug-in takes over on the server-side code and generates an HTML response for the Web server to send back to the client. As we will see, Microsoft's IIS Web server and the ASP.NET runtime work in exactly this fashion.

Internet Information Services (IIS)

IIS is a powerful Web server designed specifically to both handle ordinary HTML and act as a framework for other runtime modules such as ASP.NET. In fact, you can add runtimes to IIS for all sorts of Web technologies, including PHP, JSP, CGI-BIN, and others. For more details on the plug-in options for IIS, see ⚙JS050004. For now, we will focus on using IIS with ASP.NET.

IIS Engine Mappings
If you have installed the .NET Framework (installation instructions can be found in Chapter 2), you can see IIS's routing characteristics by going to your control panel and opening **Administrative Tools** → **Internet Information Services.** This will invoke Internet Information Services (Figure 5.6), which allows you to peruse and customize various settings, such as security.

Right-click **Default Web Site,** select **Properties,** and click the **Home Directories** tab. Now click **Configuration,** which will bring up a list of application mappings, as shown in Figure 5.7.

Application mappings inform IIS which engine to run whenever a user requests a page with a specific file extension. If you scroll down the list to .aspx (the new file extension in ASP.NET), you will see that its associated engine ("executable path" in IIS terminology) is as follows:

```
\%winroot%\Microsoft.NET\Framework\%sdk_version%\
aspnet_isapi.dll
```

Listing 5.3 The ASP.NET engine mapping

Based on our investigation, we can make two observations:

- Essential .NET Framework files such as the ASP.NET engine are found in the \%winroot%\Microsoft.NET\Framework\%sdk_version%\ directory. If you look inside this directory, you will find a number of other files required by ASP.NET.

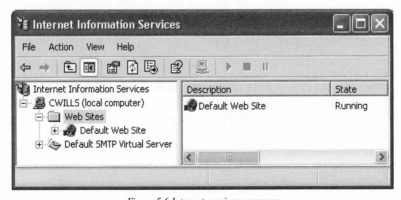

Figure 5.6 Internet services manager

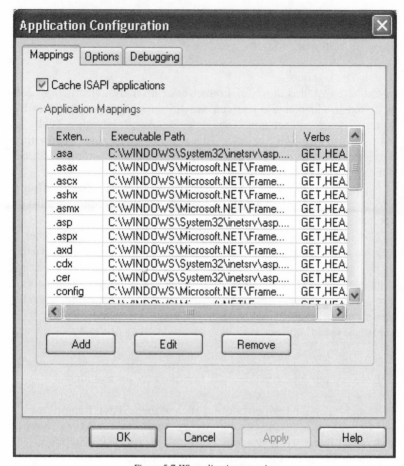

Figure 5.7 IIS application mapping

- A number of other file extensions are also associated with the
  ASP.NET engine. For example, .asmx files (which denote Web
  Services) are also processed through ASP.NET.

In addition to routing HTTP requests to their appropriate engines, IIS
provides important infrastructure to ASP.NET applications such as ad-
ministration, HTTP error handling, and security.

Required IIS Versions
ASP.NET must run under IIS version 5.0 or later. A by-product of this
requirement is that ASP.NET will only run on the Windows 2000 and

XP operating systems. Table 5.1 lists each operating system and the version of IIS with which it is packaged.

Basic Operating System	Default IIS Version
Windows NT 4.0 (with the Option Pack) IIS 4.0	IIS 4.0
Windows 2000 Professional, Server, Advanced Server	IIS 5.0
Windows XP Professional	IIS 5.1
Windows Server 2003	IIS 6.0

Table 5.1 Microsoft Operating System and IIS versions

IIS 6.0, which is available with Windows Server 2003, improves significantly upon existing versions of IIS (particularly in the areas of security, performance, and stability).

ASP.NET Runtime

As we have seen, IIS is the front gatekeeper for all HTTP requests. Whenever an ASP.NET request is received, IIS maps the extension to the ASP.NET runtime and transfers control. The ASP.NET runtime processes the appropriate page or Web Service, generates an HTTP response, and passes it back to IIS, which, in turn, passes the response back to the client.

Consider the simple ASP.NET application shown in Listing 5.4 (yes, it really can be this simple).

```
<%
  Response.Write("Hello World!");
%>
```

Listing 5.4 simple.aspx—a simple ASP.NET application

In this case, when the browser requests simple.aspx, the Web server recognizes the extension and transfers control to the ASP.NET runtime. The ASP.NET runtime interprets Listing 5.4 and generates client-side HTML to display "Hello World" in the user's browser. In addition to producing output that is rendered on a browser, a runtime must also take care of details such as maintaining application state and enforcing security. The ASP.NET runtime engine is responsible for compiling an application's CodeBehind file and supporting J# code into MSIL before executing it.

Topic: Visual Studio .NET and ASP.NET

In this topic we examine two important aspects of creating Web Applications using Visual Studio .NET: automation and design. Every time you create an ASP.NET project in VS .NET, the IDE implicitly performs a number of important administrative steps behind the scenes. Although these details are transparent when developing in VS .NET, they become important if you decide to develop outside the environment or want to deploy an application to a Web server. In this topic, we will show you what is happening behind the scenes and how much work VS .NET does for you.

In the preceding section of this topic we examined some of the VS .NET design features that you can apply to Web Applications. Many of these design features are actually quite similar to the material covered in Chapter 4 on Windows Forms. Not only are the drag-and-drop design processes similar in using Windows Forms and Web Forms, but many of the underlying concepts are identical.

CONCEPTS

The Files behind a Project

An ASP.NET application must reside in an IIS virtual directory. A *virtual directory* is a link created in the Web server that maps a uniform resource locator (URL) to a physical directory on the hard drive. In addition, a virtual directory allows all the files within the directory to share resources such as Application and Session variables (used for maintaining state in a Web Application), common code made available through global application files, and more. Therefore, if two ASP.NET scripts (script1.aspx and script2.aspx) are placed in different virtual directories, they will not be able to share such resources.

When you create a new J# ASP.NET Web Application, as demonstrated in the simple application, VS .NET allows you to specify the location of the project, as shown in Figure 5.8. The machine where the application is created (the Location box in Figure 5.8) will differ depending on your configuration settings. If the Web server (IIS) resides on your machine (common during the development stage), then the lo-

Figure 5.8 Web project location

cation will be localhost, as in Figure 5.8. If the Web server resides on a different machine (e.g., if you are developing against a production server), the location will be the name or IP address of the remote machine.

By default, a Web Application project created in VS .NET contains a number of files, all of which are listed in the Solution Explorer (Figure 5.9), which you can find in the top right corner of VS .NET. The files in Figure 5.9, which we will explain in a moment, constitute the Web Application. When VS .NET created the project, it *created an IIS virtual directory with the same name as the application.* Thus, on the Web server (on either the local or the remote machine), you can find an IIS virtual directory named MyApplication. Most often, this directory will map to the directory c:\inetpub\wwwroot\MyApplication on the machine (where c:\ is the drive where the OS is installed). Within this virtual directory, VS .NET creates the following files:

- AssemblyInfo.jsl   This file, found in all VS .NET templates, contains a collection of common attributes that provides the compiler with specific instructions on how to compile an application (assembly details, version information, etc.). Note that we have not yet introduced the concept of .NET *attributes* in this book; you will learn about attributes in Chapter 6. You will rarely modify AssemblyInfo.jsl when you develop a Web project, as its contents are generally used for informational purposes not applicable in the context of a Web Application.
- Web.config   This file houses the project's configuration settings. The settings in this file determine options such as application tracing, session storage, and security. Load this file in VS .NET's code editor (by double-clicking it in the Solution Explorer) and you will see that it is in XML format. Although the contents of Web.config are beyond the scope of this CodeNotes, you can find more information on configuring a Web Application using Web.config at ⌖JS050020.

Figure 5.9 Default project files

- Webform1.aspx Anytime you create a new Web Application project in VS .NET, the environment gives the project a default Web Form named WebForm1.aspx. In practice, you would likely rename Webform1.aspx to something more appropriate. In the majority of examples in this book we will simply use this default form. You can add Web Forms to an application by selecting **Add Web Form** from the **Project** menu in VS .NET. All Web Forms in a project will be listed in the Solution Explorer, and you can move between them simply by clicking on the Web Form names.

- Global.asax This file is used to declare objects and events that can be used by every file in your application. The Global.asax file contains three main entities:

  o *Event declarations.* If you peer inside this file you will find handler methods such as Application_Start() and Session_Start(), which allow you to write code that is called when the Web Application is initially requested by anyone and when the application is first requested by a particular user. Other handler methods in this file allow you to respond to other events such as application-wide errors and the unloading of the application. The events in this file trigger when *any* page in the application is requested. For example, if you want to perform an operation the first time a user accesses any page in the application, you write code in the Session_Start() event handler method. You'll learn more about sessions and the Session object later in this topic.

  o *Namespace references.* Within the Global.asax file you can implicitly reference namespaces (using the import keyword). If you look at the top of Global.asax, you will find the four lines shown in Listing 5.5.

```
import System.Collections.*;
import System.ComponentModel.*;
import System.Web.*;
import System.Web.SessionState.*;
```

Listing 5.5 Importing namespaces into Global.asax

The important point is that namespaces that are referenced in this file apply to *all* pages in the application. Thus, if you wanted to utilize the Framework's XML classes throughout a J# Web Application, you would include the line imports System.XML.* at the top of Global.asax. (Remember from Chapter 3, however, that to use Framework classes you must not only reference the namespace, but also include a reference to the Framework assembly using VS .NET's **Add Reference** menu option.)

- ○ *Server-side includes and object tag declarations.* A server-side include allows ASP.NET to "paste" code from external files into Global.asax, thus making the external files' contents accessible to all pages in the application. For example, by placing the line shown in Listing 5.6 in Global.asax, the contents of MyFunction.dat become globally accessible.

```
<!-- #include File = "MyFunction.dat" -->
```

Listing 5.6 A server-side include

You can also place object tag declarations inside Global.asax, which instruct the framework to create .NET assemblies on the fly on an application or user basis. For examples of both server-side includes and object tags, please see ⊶JS050020.

Bear in mind that an ASP.NET application does not require any of these files (with the exception of a basic .aspx file). As we will see later in this chapter, however, these files (particularly web.config) greatly simplify configuration and deployment.

Inside an ASP.NET Application

If we keep in mind our discussions of assemblies and the .NET Framework from Chapter 1, we can state the following two important facets of ASP.NET's architecture:

- ASP.NET itself is exposed through the BCL found in the System. Web namespace (and other namespaces within it such as System. Web.UI).
- ASP.NET applications are compiled into assemblies. The ASP. NET runtime uses assemblies to generate client-side HTML, to process user input, and to respond to user requests. In fact, the ASP.NET runtime is itself an assembly that runs under the control of IIS.

Assuming you created the MyApplication ASP.NET project we dealt with in the preceding section, click on the HTML tab that appears at the bottom left of its Design window, as shown in Figure 5.10. The HTML code you see is the *server-side* HTML for the current page. You will rarely need to edit the HTML code for a Web Form manually, because the Web Forms Designer writes HTML for you. However, it is helpful to understand what is being generated behind the scenes when you drag controls onto a Web Form. The HTML code you will see after clicking the HTML tab represents the application's graphical representation in a browser. Remember that *client-side* HTML will be generated by the ASP.NET runtime on the fly and will be different, depending on the browser the user is using. Let's look more closely at some of the features of this server-side code.

The Page Directive
Look at the top of the HTML for MyApplication's WebForm1.aspx and you will find the line of code shown in Listing 5.7.

```
<%@ Page language="VJ#" Codebehind="WebForm1.aspx.jsl"
AutoEventWireup="false"
Inherits="myApplication.WebForm1" %>
```

Listing 5.7 The Page directive

What you are seeing is an important entity in ASP.NET called the Page directive, which describes certain characteristics of the Web Form to the ASP.NET runtime. For example, the Language attribute in the Page directive tells ASP.NET which compiler to use on scripts in the .aspx file (in this case, the J# compiler). More important, however, is the Code-Behind attribute that tells VS .NET where the application's associated logic is located.

Remember, an important aspect of ASP.NET is the ability to separate code from content. This is accomplished (in part) by the CodeBehind attribute. To see CodeBehind in action, flip back to the page's GUI by clicking the **Design** icon (Figure 5.10), and add a Button to the application by dragging it from the toolbox. Double-click the Button you added and VS .NET will bring up the WebForm1.aspx.jsl file that contains the

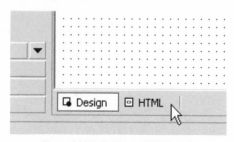

Figure 5.10 Switching to HTML mode

page's underlying code. From this exercise, we can see that our Web Application consists of two main files:

- WebForm1.aspx   The page's design. This file contains the server-side HTML that describes the Web Controls that are being used, client- or server-side script that you directly add to this file, and any other design elements such as Image references or Cascading Style Sheets (CSS).
- WebForm1.aspx.jsl   The page's logic. This file uses certain .NET Framework classes that map to each element in the design file. It also stores the code that you write to respond to events triggered on the design page. By convention, the CodeBehind file has the same name as the design file, with an added language extension (.jsl, in this case).

Thus, by using the CodeBehind attribute, which establishes a relationship between the design file and the code file, ASP.NET can keep these aspects of your application separate.

The CodeBehind File

The application's logic file (WebForm1.aspx.jsl) contains some interesting code that we have ignored up to this point. Specifically, consider the lines given in Listing 5.8.

```
public class WebForm1 extends System.Web.UI.Page
{
  protected System.Web.UI.WebControls.Button Button1;
  //remaining code removed for brevity
}
```

Listing 5.8 WebForm1.aspx.jsl

Based on our discussion of the .NET Framework Libraries in the previous topics, you can see that Listing 5.8 uses classes found in the System.Web.UI and System.Web.UI.WebControls namespaces. The Button1 class (and other Web Control classes) will be covered in the next topic of this chapter. For now, let's take a closer look at the System.Web.UI.Page class.

The Page Class

In ASP.NET a Web Form is encapsulated by a Page class. Thus, if an application contains a Web Form named Webform1, its CodeBehind file declares a class that *inherits* from the Page class found in the System.Web.UI namespace, as shown in Listing 5.9.

```
public class WebForm1 extends System.Web.UI.Page
```

Listing 5.9 Inheriting from the **Page** *class*

Web Applications can have as many forms as you like, and each one extends the BCL `Page` class. If you're unclear about the concept of inheritance, please consult Chapter 3 before continuing.

Again, we can draw analogies between Web Forms and Windows Forms. Just as a Windows application `Form` object exposes events such as `Form_Load()` and `Form_Initialize()`, the `Page` class (and, hence, the `WebForm1` class) exposes events such as `Page_Load()` and `Page_Init()`. Thus, if you wanted to execute some code when a Web Form loaded (to initialize database connections, for example), you would place it in the `Page_Load()` event.

Code Generation and the Web Forms Designer
Both the `Page` and the `Button` classes in Listing 5.8 are found in the .NET Framework. Yet how, exactly, did the lines of code shown in Listing 5.8 get in the source code in the first place? The answer is the Windows Forms Designer (WFD) that we discussed in Chapter 4.

When you draw a button or textbox onto a Web Form, the WFD translates your actions into J# code that calls the classes found in the `System.Web` and other namespaces. This code then becomes an integral part of the `CodeBehind` file, to which you can add your own logic.

Remember that the Framework Libraries exist as language-neutral IL code. These classes are thus callable from any language that targets the .NET Framework. However, in order for the WFD to generate code automatically, the language must support special Microsoft "Code Generation" extensions.

In large part, you can ignore such details and simply program in the manner we have illustrated. That having been said, it is educational and revealing to consider the trickery that ASP.NET is performing behind the scenes. We will relegate the majority of this discussion to ⓒⓃ⃗JS050005; however, one practical implementation detail is how ASP.NET compiles your applications.

The Compilation Process
When a user requests an `.aspx` file for the first time, the ASP.NET runtime performs two important operations:

1. It compiles the `CodeBehind` file into an assembly (if the file hasn't already been compiled either by you or by VS .NET).

2. It creates a second assembly called a `Page` class, which is a combination of the design file (`.aspx`) and the `CodeBehind` assembly produced in the first step. Think of the `Page` class as an executable file that accepts incoming requests, processes them according to your application's logic, and returns results to the user. (Don't confuse this compiled `Page` class with the .NET Framework `Page` class in Listing 5.9.)

An important aspect of ASP.NET's compilation process is that Step 2 is performed only when the page is initially requested; subsequent requests execute against an already existing `Page` class. ASP.NET actually caches `Page` class assemblies (in `%winroot%\Microsoft.NET\Framework\ vX.xxx\Temporary ASP.NET Files`) in order to improve performance. You can find more detailed information on ASP.NET's compilation process at ⟲ JS050006.

The Web Form Paradigm

The best thing about Web Application development using ASP.NET is that it can be almost exactly like developing Windows applications, as discussed in Chapter 4. In fact, if you are entirely new to Visual Studio .NET development, you may not even notice a difference. When you add a control (called a *Web Control* in ASP.NET), VS .NET creates an object to represent the control and generates an event handler method, just as it does for normal Windows applications. However, because ASP.NET applications must also be accessible over the Web, VS .NET takes on the extra job of generating code that represents the controls you draw and configure as HTML.

In this section, we'll examine the Web Form paradigm, in which Visual Studio .NET must simultaneously generate J# code and HTML code for Web Controls added to a GUI. Before getting into the Web Form paradigm, however, we need to take a short sidetrack and look more closely at HTTP, the key protocol behind the World Wide Web. If you haven't read the discussion on HTTP in the "Core Concepts" section in this chapter, we recommend that you go back and do so before continuing.

HTTP

The Internet is data-centric—to obtain information, you usually have to provide it. To perform an Internet search, for example, you must provide the subject of the search. In HTTP, this information is communicated as *name-value pairs:* the name of the variable being sent (in our case it might be `SearchSubject`) and the contents of the variable (which might be "CodeNotes").

HTTP defines two procedures for transmitting data over the Internet—namely, HTTP GET and HTTP POST. The difference between these two protocols lies in the way these name-value pairs are transported.

- **HTTP GET**   In an HTTP GET request, name-value pairs are transmitted as part of the URL request itself. If you were to perform a search for "CodeNotes" on the popular Google™ Internet search site, for example, the address that appeared in the address bar of your browser would look similar to Listing 5.10.

```
http://www.google.com/search?q=CodeNotes
```

Listing 5.10 A GET request

Notice the name-value pair in the preceding URL (sometimes called a QueryString value). The "q" represents the name of the variable. The value associated with "q" is our search string, "CodeNotes." HTTP GET requests are formed in the preceding format by appending name-value pairs to the URL request, a process commonly referred to as *URL-encoding*.

- **HTTP POST**   Similar to GET, HTTP POST sends name-value pairs to a destination on the Internet. The difference is that name-value pairs are not appended to the destination URL, but are instead embedded in the HTTP message body. When you fill out a customer information form online with information such as your name and credit card number, POST is often used instead of GET. By using POST, transmitted data is packaged in the message body and does not appear in the URL, affording a greater amount of security.

As we will see in this topic, the Web Form paradigm is based almost exclusively on the POST mechanism (although you can still use GET if you wish).

Form Design in ASP.NET
ASP.NET is based almost exclusively on the event model we demonstrated in Chapter 4. As with a Windows application, every entity in an ASP.NET application—a Button, a TextBox, even a Web page itself—is really an instance of a class in the BCL. When a Web Form is accessed for the first time, ASP.NET instantiates all the classes representing the entities within the page.

You don't need to know any HTML at all to manipulate the appearance of an ASP.NET Web Form (although some basic knowledge of HTML always helps). Instead, you can simply drag and drop controls into the Design window and then change their appearances using the Properties browser (e.g., to change a control's color, modify its BackColor property). Similarly, to respond to an event such as the click of a button, you don't have to worry about POST or GET or HTML forms; you simply write code into the object's event handler (such as Button1_Click).

For example, try dragging a Checkbox control and a TextBox onto a Web Form, as in Figure 5.11. This action actually generates server-side HTML to represent these two components. Later, this HTML will be translated into client-side HTML that will render correctly in any browser. If you want to see the HTML representing the CheckBox and the TextBox you just created, click on the **HTML** tab at the bottom of the Design window and you will see two lines that look like Listing 5.11 (line breaks added for readability).

```
<asp:CheckBox id="CheckBox1" style="Z-INDEX: 101; LEFT: 264px;
 POSITION: absolute; TOP: 176px"
 runat="server"></asp:CheckBox>
<asp:TextBox id="TextBox1" style="Z-INDEX: 102; LEFT: 288px;
 POSITION: absolute; TOP: 232px"
 runat="server"></asp:TextBox>
```

Listing 5.11 Server-side HTML generated by Visual Studio .NET

Next, switch back to the design view (click on the **Design** tab next to the HTML tab) and double-click the CheckBox to open its CodeBehind. Notice that VS .NET opens a file named MyApplication.aspx.jsl— CodeBehind for Web Forms will always have this double extension. Type the bold code in Listing 5.12 inside the Checkbox1_CheckChanged() event handler.

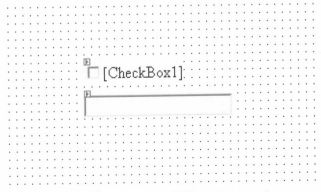

Figure 5.11 CheckBox and TextBox Web Controls

```
private void CheckBox1_CheckedChanged (Object sender,
  System.EventArgs e)
{
  TextBox1.set_Text("Status of CheckBox: " +
  CheckBox1.get_Checked());
}
```

Listing 5.12 Responding to a CheckBox click

Before running the application, return to the design view (click on the **WebForm1.aspx** tab) and change the CheckBox1.AutoPostBack property to True using the Property browser (we'll examine the role of Auto-PostBack in the following section). Remember that you have to click on the CheckBox to select it before its properties will be available.

Run the application by pressing the **CTRL + F5** key (just like a Windows application!). It will open in a Web browser. Try clicking on the CheckBox—you will see that every time you do so, the code in Listing 5.12 will execute and alter the TextBox's contents. We could have followed exactly the same steps in a J# Windows application and achieved virtually identical results.

Postback

In a Windows application, all forms have *state*. When you click a button in a J# Windows application, you have some expectations about what will happen. You expect that the current form will stay visible. You expect that all the data you have inserted into the various fields (textboxes, checkboxes, etc.) will remain in those fields. In other words, you expect that the Windows Form will *maintain its state*.

Unlike Windows Forms, Web Applications traditionally do *not* have state. When you click on a link in an HTML page, a new page loads (or the current page is reloaded), and the contents of other fields on the page are generally either lost or must be manually reinserted into the fields. However, in order to allow ASP.NET Web Applications to be developed exactly like Windows Forms applications, ASP.NET gives Web Applications the illusion of state using a mechanism called POSTBACK.

Suppose we have a Web Application with some textboxes a user is expected to fill out and a button that submits the information in those textboxes using an HTTP POST. In normal Web development (using server-side script), the POST request would be to another page, and that page would perform some operations on the gathered data and return results to the client.

However, suppose you wanted to submit the information to the Web server instead, so that it could be processed by some back-end code rather than another Web page. You would want to return to your original page rather than going someplace new. For example, you might want to validate data the user has entered against information in a database. If the user's information does not match what is in the database, you could display an error message on the original page and indicate which textboxes were incorrectly filled out. "Posting back" to the same page in this way allows you to perform server-side operations *before* moving on to the next appropriate ASP.NET page. Thanks to the way ASP.NET handles this process, your user won't even have to fill out the correct data again!

For example, suppose we had an .aspx page named Login.aspx that executes a POSTBACK. The HTML element representing this form might look like Listing 5.13.

```
<form name="loginForm" method="post" action="WebForm1.aspx"
id="Form1">
```

Listing 5.13 The Login POST action

This element dictates that when a "submit" action occurs on the page (e.g., a button is pressed that submits the form), the information gathered for the form will post to the current page.

The process of a self-POST (often referred to as a POSTBACK), may seem complex but it is really quite simple:

1. The first time Login.aspx is requested, no page information (TextBox values, form values, hidden fields, etc.) accompanies the request. All the fields are blank.
2. When the user clicks the **Submit** button after filling out the data, Login.aspx is requested a second time from the Web server. However, the second request is accompanied by page information, such as the values of the TextBox controls.

In ASP.NET, the POSTBACK technique takes place mostly automatically, underneath the hood. That is, when the user performs an action that warrants the execution of server-side code, the Web Form posts back to itself to run the code you wrote in your CodeBehind file, unless you have indicated differently.

Remember that all the page information is also included with the POSTBACK request. For an ASP.NET Web Form, this information includes the following:

• A hidden field called VIEWSTATE that maintains the state of the page's Web Controls. We'll examine this field in greater depth in the next topic of this chapter.

- The contents of the page's Web Controls, such as TextBox and ListBox values.
- Other boilerplate information that ASP.NET embeds in the request, such as hidden EVENTTARGET and EVENTARGUMENT fields, which we will examine shortly.

All of this information is utilized by ASP.NET to facilitate its object programming model on the server. For example, as we will see in the next topic, it is the VIEWSTATE field that allows a Web Control's appearance to be easily manipulated through intuitive properties such as BackColor.

Please note that all POSTBACK operations in ASP.NET occur automatically; in most cases, you won't ever have to worry about making sure your Web Form's state will be maintained after the user activates a button (or any other Web Control). The only time you need to pay attention to POSTBACK at all is if you want to change the default behavior of a Web Control so that it will execute a POSTBACK when it normally does not, or not execute a POSTBACK when it normally does. Changing the POSTBACK behavior of a Web Control is accomplished by manipulating its AutoPostBack property.

The AutoPostBack Property

By default, most Web Controls automatically trigger a page POST-BACK. Some simpler controls that do not have server-side code, such as textboxes, labels, and checkboxes, do not, by default, trigger a POSTBACK. POSTBACK behavior is determined through a control's Auto-PostBack property, which, when set to True, forces ASP.NET to perform a POSTBACK when the control is activated. You can set a Web Control's AutoPostBack property by clicking on the control and then modifying the AutoPostBack property found in the Properties browser. Try setting AutoPostBack to true for the CheckBox and TextBox in Figure 5.11, and then add the code in Listing 5.14 to the TextBox1_TextChanged event handler (double-click on the TextBox to open the CodeBehind and create the TextChanged handler).

```
private void TextBox1_TextChanged (Object sender,
 System.EventArgs e)
{
 textBox1.set_Text(""+ textBox1.get_TextLength());
}
```

Listing 5.14 The TextBox_TextChanged() *event*

The code in Listing 5.14 is triggered when the contents of the TextBox change. Run the application, and enter something into the

TextBox (such as "Hello"). Next, tab off the control such that it loses focus, and the page will automatically post back to the server. The code in Listing 5.14 will execute and the contents of the TextBox will change to report the length of the string you entered (5, in our case).

Those familiar with Web development may wonder how ASP.NET determines which control triggers the POSTBACK. For example, in Figure 5.11, both the CheckBox control and the TextBox are capable of posting back to the server (because we changed both AutoPostBack properties to True). How does ASP.NET figure out "who did it"?

If you examine the HTML source that ASP.NET generates for the Web page in Figure 5.11, you will find two hidden HTML fields that ASP.NET employs for this purpose: EVENTTARGET and EVENTARGUMENT. These two fields provide all the information ASP.NET needs to keep track of which entity launched the event and what event was fired. The internal use of these fields is beyond the scope of this book, but for a more involved examination please see °⚙ JS050007.

It should be apparent why the POSTBACK architecture is employed by ASP.NET—among other things, it allows the framework to utilize hidden fields such as VIEWSTATE and EVENTTARGET that facilitate the intuitive object model that we have illustrated.

Intrinsic Objects

ASP.NET provides several important objects called *intrinsic objects* that are often needed when developing Web Applications. You can call methods on intrinsic objects to manipulate the contents of HTTP messages going to and from the server, as well as the state of an application (explained subsequently).

We will discuss the four most important intrinsic objects you will encounter when developing in ASP.NET: Response, Request, Session, and Application. Note that in J#, intrinsic objects must be obtained and updated using set_ and get_ accessor methods, since J# does not directly support properties like C# and VB.NET.

Request

The Request object is used primarily to access the contents of the HTTP request that was sent to the current page. For example, suppose we used the HTTP GET request in Listing 5.15 to access a particular page.

```
http://localhost/myWebApp/WebForm1.aspx?name=Bob@age=42
```

Listing 5.15 A simple GET request

We can access the two parameters in this URL via the Request object as shown in Listing 5.16.

```
String username = get_Request().get_Params()
.get_Item("name");
```

Listing 5.16 Accessing Request *parameters*

Listing 5.16 will assign the value "Bob" to a new String variable named username. However, our code has no idea what this value will be until we access the HTTP request using the Request intrinsic object.

Behind the scenes, the get_Request() method actually returns an instance of System.Web.HttpRequest. However, you will almost always deal with this class as shown in Listing 5.16.

Response

This object represents the HTTP response your page generates when it processes an HTTP request. You can use the Response object to add content to this response message. The simplest and most common use of the Response object is to write text output directly to a page, as in Listing 5.17.

```
get_Response().Write("Hi there!");
```

Listing 5.17 Using the Response *object*

You can think of the Write() method as being similar to the println() method in a console application, except that Write() prints the string to a Web page instead of to the console. Note that you can also put HTML tags in a Write() statement to format the strings you are printing to the Web browser, as in Listing 5.18.

```
get_Response().Write("<h1>Hi there!</h1>");
```

Listing 5.18 Using Write() *with HTML*

Once again, get_Response() actually returns an instance of System. Web.HTTPResponse, although you will rarely need to work with this object directly.

Session

Each user who accesses your Web Application will have his or her own session. The *session* is used to keep track of user-specific information; it is inaccessible to anyone but the session owner. Using the Session object, you can store data in a user's session, which can then be retrieved anytime, on any other page of your application. This is one way of transferring user data between pages in an application.

The Session object keeps track of information as sets of name-value pairs. For example, Listing 5.19 adds a username item to the session with a value of "Craig".

```
get_Session().Add("username","Craig");
```

Listing 5.19 Adding a name-value pair to the session

Now, the username variable can be accessed for the current user from anywhere else in the application, as long as the user's current session doesn't end, as in Listing 5.20.

```
get_Response().Write(get_Session() .get_Item("username"));
```

Listing 5.20 Accessing the session

Note that the name of a session item must be a string, but the value of the session item can be any object.

As the Web Application designer, you have complete control over how a session is handled, including when it begins and ends and how long it will last after the user leaves the site. For more information on session handling in ASP.NET applications, please see ☜JS050008.

Application

The Application object is like the Session object, except that items stored in it are available to all users of your Web Application. The Application object is stored in the ASP.NET runtime process, so information stored within it will last until your application shuts down. If you are familiar with static variables in Java, you can think of items stored in Application as being static and items stored in Session as being instance-specific.

The Application object (actually System.Web.HttpApplication) uses the same name-value pair structure as Session and is accessed in the same fashion, only using the get/set_Application() accessors instead of get/set_Session().

Web Page Design in VS .NET

The primary virtue of ASP.NET is that Web-based applications can be designed using the Windows Form Designer that we used to develop Windows applications in Chapter 4. For Web Applications, the WFD produces the appropriate server-side HTML and Web Control declarations behind the scenes. For the most part, application development in ASP.NET can be done entirely using the WFD, and you won't have to worry about any other Web technologies directly. Nevertheless, there are a number of mature Web-related technologies that can be integrated with the framework's Web Form paradigm:

- **Client-side script.** Web Control code (the code generated by the WFD for ASP.NET applications) executes entirely on the server. However, scripting languages such as JavaScript can be used to execute code on the client side (that is, in the user's Web browser) before a Web Control's server-side code runs. You can add JavaScript to a Web Form's design file (.aspx).

- **Cascading Style Sheets (CSS)** Cascading Style Sheets are documents used by Web designers to apply styles (such as fonts, colors, and sizes) to elements on a Web page. CSS allows you to group one or more design elements under the umbrella of a single entity and then apply that entity to as many elements as you like on a page. In this way, when you wish to apply a design change to the project (a color adjustment, for example), you can apply the change to the single entity, and the modification will cascade to its related elements. To learn how to use CSS in a J# Web Application, see ᵒ⤷JS050009.

- **Frames** Frames allow you to divide the client's browser window into independent subwindows, each with its own characteristics and set of scrollbars. Each window can also be made resizable, so that users can customize the size of the frames. With VS .NET, it is possible to utilize frames such that each subwindow displays a different Web Form (.aspx) in the project. This requires adding a Frameset entity to the Web Application and configuring it appropriately. We detail this procedure at ᵒ⤷JS050010.

- **User Controls** One of the biggest challenges in Web development is the sharing of code between multiple pages. As mentioned earlier, one way of doing this is a server-side include. A server-side include (discussed in the previous Global.asax explanation) simply "pastes" the contents of an external file into the target file. Often, this technique results in cumbersome and unwieldy code, and leads to problems such as name collisions and nested include file complexity.

    User controls are a powerful alternative to server-side includes in ASP.NET. A user control allows you to group overlapping functionality into one file (with an .ascx extension), which can then be included into those pages that you designate. For example, if there is a company header that must be on every page in a project, you can place it within the auspices of a user control and simply include the control on the desired forms. Because a user control is logically isolated from the rest of the project, problems that arise with server-side includes are eliminated. For more information on user controls see ᵒ⤷JS050011.

For more information on these technologies and how they can be used to enhance a Web Application, please see *CodeNotes for Web-Based UI.*

EXAMPLE

The next topic in this chapter will provide an overview of many of the commonly used Web Controls in ASP.NET applications. As you have not yet been exposed to many of these controls, a more complex example might be difficult at this point without introducing a lot of new information. For this reason, Chapter 5 will contain only one example, and you can find it in the "Example" section at the end of the next topic.

HOW AND WHY

How Can I Use CSS in an ASP.NET Page?

Cascading Style Sheets (CSS) is used to maintain a common look and feel throughout a website or Web Application. CSS syntax allows you to create "classes" of design information such as font styles and sizes, colors, and paragraph formatting. By referencing a CSS stylesheet from an HTML (or ASP.NET) page, you gain access to these classes and can apply them to your HTML elements using a special `class` attribute.

J# ASP.NET applications can be linked to CSS stylesheets using the **Format → Document Styles** dialog. This dialog allows you to design new styles for your Web Application pages or link an existing CSS stylesheet to your current application. See ⟨CN⟩JS050009 for more information on using CSS with ASP.NET.

What Are Cookies?

A cookie is a small piece of information that is obtained and stored in a client's browser. Generally, cookies are used to maintain information about various websites the user has visited, such as login information or user preferences. For example, if you have a Hotmail account, you may be familiar with the option it gives you to "Sign me in automatically." When you select this option and log in, Hotmail sends a cookie to your browser, which it keeps in a special directory on your hard drive. This cookie contains your (encrypted) login information. The next time you access Hotmail, the website will ask your browser if it has the "sign me in automatically" cookie. If your browser has the cookie, it will use the information from the cookie to log you into Hotmail and you won't have to type your name and password again manually.

ASP.NET uses cookies primarily when dealing with user sessions. It stores the session ID in a cookie on the user's machine, so that the ID can be recalled at a later date and linked to the right information on the server. Although most of ASP.NET's cookie usage is done behind the scenes, you may find that you want to create and store your own cookies on a user's browser as well. To learn how to do this, please see ↻JS050012.

DESIGN NOTES

ASP.NET Development Is Desktop Development
When writing applications in ASP.NET, it helps to think increasingly in terms of traditional desktop development. For example, to toggle the visibility of a graphical element in ASP.NET, you simply modify the control's `Visible` property just as you do for Windows desktop applications. Behind the scenes, the framework alters the generated HTML appropriately.

ASP.NET Starter Kits
Microsoft has developed a complete set of starter applications in ASP.NET. These applications cover a range of common Web Applications including forums, e-commerce, and information portals. Although the Starter Kits were originally developed in C# and VB.NET, J# versions are now available from www.asp.net/starterkits. You can download a VS .NET version or a version that will work with Web Matrix. The Starter Kits are intended to be reference applications that you can dissect, modify, and enhance as you please while learning the intricacies of ASP.NET.

SUMMARY

Working with Web Forms in ASP.NET is, on the surface, exactly like working with Windows Forms. You drag and drop a component into the Design window, configure it using the Properties browser, and then write code in its event handler(s) that will execute when the component is activated (and that triggers an event). Underneath the hood, ASP.NET is actually generating server-side HTML code to represent each Web Control. When you run an ASP.NET application, it is compiled into an assembly that is made available to users over the Web. When a user accesses your application, ASP.NET generates client-side HTML code appropriate to the specific client browser and browser version.

ASP.NET is architecturally based on the HTTP POSTBACK mechanism whereby Web Forms post to themselves to trigger application events such as the click of a button or the modification of a TextBox. The POST architecture is appropriate for ASP.NET because a POST maintains page information such as control values and hidden fields in between server requests. This information is used internally by ASP.NET to facilitate its intuitive object model that you program against.

You can detect whether a Web Form is posting back to itself using the Page.get_IsPostBack()method. This Boolean method allows you to perform specific operations only when the Web Form is initially requested, allowing you to reduce response time when the page posts back thereafter.

Remember that even though the HTML code generated by VS .NET doesn't look like traditional HTML, you can treat it the same way. Web technologies with which you may be familiar, such as JavaScript, CSS, and frames, can all be applied to ASP.NET pages. In general, however, you can design ASP.NET Web Applications without ever having to edit the HTML manually, just by sticking with the Web Control and event handler paradigm.

Topic: Web Controls and Web Forms

Web Controls are one of the primary technologies behind ASP.NET's intuitive design process. A Web Control is just like any other BCL class, only it has some peculiar behaviors. Specifically, a Web Control normally acts just like the Windows Form controls from Chapter 4. However, when a client requests an ASP.NET page, the ASP.NET transforms the Web Control into HTML for delivery in the HTTP response. In other words, the reason you can drag and drop controls on ASP.NET and do not need to know HTML is that the ASP.NET runtime takes care of the HTML transformation for you.

An ASP.NET application is, to a large extent, a construction of interacting Web Controls. There are over 60 Web Controls in the framework, and you can easily extend these controls or write your own. In this topic, we will look at ASP.NET's Web Control architecture and examine some of the more interesting Web Controls.

CONCEPTS

Defining the Term Web Control
You will often see the terms *Web Control, server control,* and *Web Form control* used interchangeably. Because Web Controls are first processed

on the server by the ASP.NET runtime, they are sometimes referred to as *server controls*. What is potentially confusing (and sometimes obscured by the documentation) is that the term *Web Controls* actually encompasses two different sets of controls:

1. *Web Form controls.* All of the controls we demonstrate in this chapter are Web Form controls. These controls emulate the object model and properties of controls found in Windows Form applications. The terminology from Chapter 4, such as *handlers, events,* and *properties,* applies to Web Form controls. The important point to remember with respect to these controls is that, often, Web Form controls don't have direct mappings to HTML elements. For example, HTML syntax does not contain a calendar element. Thus, the Calendar Web Form control must be reproduced on the client as a combination of HTML tables and JavaScript. Thanks to the ASP.NET runtime and .NET Framework, however, you don't need to know any HTML or JavaScript to build an application with a sophisticated calendar control. In general, most of the controls you will use in ASP.NET will be Web Form controls.

2. *HTML server controls.* Like Web Form controls, HTML server controls are processed on the server before they are rendered on the client. The difference between Web Form and HTML server controls is that HTML server controls map directly to simple HTML elements and are manipulated in accordance with the conventions of HTML. This means that
   - HTML server controls are not as feature rich as their Web Form counterparts.
   - Using HTML server controls requires that you have some familiarity with HTML.

As previously mentioned, we will deal only with Web Form controls in this book. Again, Web Form controls offer greater feature selection and are more commonly used in ASP.NET applications, especially by developers who are new to the world of Web programming. For more information on HTML server controls, please see ⟡JS050013.

Changing Control Properties

Just like the Windows Form controls from Chapter 4, the graphical Web Controls really map to classes found in the BCL. For example, create a new J# ASP.NET application and add a single TextBox to it. Then double-click on the TextBox to open the CodeBehind file, and you will see that the CodeBehind file contains the declaration in Listing 5.21.

```
protected System.Web.UI.WebControls.TextBox TextBox1;
```

Listing 5.21 Control definition

As discussed in the preceding topic, Web Controls in the design file (the .aspx file) map to instances of classes from the System.Web. UI.WebControls namespace and are contained within an .aspx.jsl CodeBehind file.

Although you will manipulate Web Form controls primarily through the Design window and Properties pane, you can also change control properties inside your code. For example, the code in Listing 5.22 changes the background color of a TextBox to dark blue when a Button control named Button1 is clicked.

```
private void Button1_Click (Object sender, System.EventArgs e)
{
 TextBox1.set_BackColor(Color.get_DarkBlue());
}
```

Listing 5.22 Changing control backgrounds

As you can see, Web Form code is quite intuitive. As with Windows Form controls, Web Form control properties are accessible through standard accessor methods (set_ and get_). The set_BackColor() method, for example, allows you to change the BackColor property.

A Survey of Web Form Controls

Space constraints do not permit us to list the capabilities and nuances of every control in the ASP.NET framework. In large part, your understanding of these controls will come through experience. For full details on each control, you can consult the documentation built into VS .NET or the MSDN Library. However, to give you an idea of the diversity and power of ASP.NET, we'll provide a brief discussion of some of the more important controls that you are likely to utilize. Some of these controls will be illustrated in the example at the end of this topic.

Basic Controls

The following controls should be self-explanatory, as they map directly to common HTML elements: HyperLink, LinkButton, Image, Panel, Label, Button, TextBox, CheckBox, RadioButton, ImageButton, Table, TableRow, and TableCell. If you're not familiar with HTML, you can find a quick refresher at ᴄᴺJS050014.

Remember that, although these entities have direct HTML equivalents, they are Web Controls that abstract HTML specifics through intuitive properties. For example, you can set the TextBox.TextMode property to Password, such that the user's keystrokes appear as asterisks instead of cleartext. Behind the scenes, the Web Control creates an HTML <input> element with an attribute of type="password".

Data Controls
Both the DataGrid and DataList controls are used in conjunction with the ADO.NET classes, which we will cover briefly in Chapter 8. Basically, these controls allow you to display and format data retrieved from a database. The DataGrid control, in particular, allows you to display the results of database queries in a sophisticated manner. For more information on these controls, see ⌗JS050015.

List Controls
As suggested by their names, CheckBoxList, DropDownList, ListBox, and RadioButtonList all allow the selection of an element within a list. One particularly important property exposed by these controls is Auto-PostBack, which determines whether the application posts back to the server automatically whenever an item in the list is selected. By default, this property is set to False. If you set it to True, then ASP.NET will generate client-side JavaScript that posts back to the server as soon as an item in the list has been selected. You can think of the AutoPostBack property as a means to turn a list selection event into the equivalent of a button click event.

   AutoPostBack is useful when the selection of an item might change the rest of the page. For example, a DropDownList may expose a number of options that determine the way a page renders (e.g., frames or no frames). Using this property you could update the page immediately when the user makes his or her selection.

Validation Controls
In many cases, you want to restrict or verify the data that a user enters into a Web Form. For example, you may want to ensure that an e-mail address matches the correct format. Fortunately, the RequiredField-Validator, CompareValidator, RangeValidator, RegularExpression-Validator, and CustomValidator controls provide a simple mechanism for performing data validation. These controls are capable of validating user input on the client (through JavaScript) if the browser supports it, or on the server if the browser is less capable. You can find more information on validation controls in the "How and Why" section near the end of this topic.

Miscellaneous Controls

The following controls don't map directly to HTML or other common components, but are often useful in ASP.NET applications.

- AdRotator This control can be used to rotate banners (images) on the top of your page (usually for advertising purposes). AdRotator has the ability to filter content through its KeyWordFilter property and the ability to configure itself based on an XML configuration file (using the AdvertisementFile property).

- Calendar This powerful control allows the user to select a date from a graphical calendar (Figure 5.12). If you add this control to a Web project and then examine the underlying client-side code that ASP.NET generates, you'll see that the Framework produces a lot of HTML and JavaScript to re-create the calendar in the browser.

  The Calendar control exposes various properties that determine how it is rendered. For example, the ShowNextPrevMonth property determines whether the user can scroll to other months. An example using the Calendar control can be found in the "Example" section later in this topic.

- XML Increasingly, Web developers are turning to XML as a means of representing data. The XML component allows you to embed an XML document directly into an ASP.NET page. This is, in itself, a powerful capability, but the XML component goes further. An important XML technology called XSLT (eXtensible Stylesheet Language Transformations) allows you to translate XML into HTML. In addition to accepting an XML file through

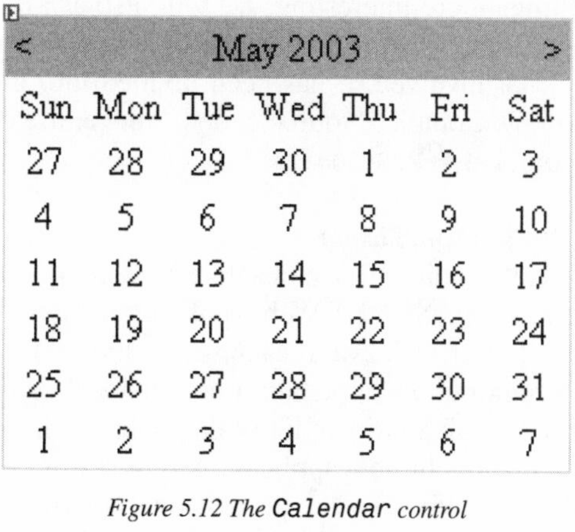

<	May 2003					>
Sun	Mon	Tue	Wed	Thu	Fri	Sat
27	28	29	30	1	2	3
4	5	6	7	8	9	10
11	12	13	14	15	16	17
18	19	20	21	22	23	24
25	26	27	28	29	30	31
1	2	3	4	5	6	7

Figure 5.12 The Calendar control

its DocumentSource property, the XML component also exposes a property called TransformSource. This optional property points to an XSLT file, which prescribes how the XML document translates into HTML, such that it can be displayed in the browser.

XML is an extremely useful component, which can result in very sophisticated ASP.NET pages. An example of this component working with XML and XSLT files can be found at o╌╍╌ JS050016.

Extending Web Controls

Remember that all the controls discussed in this topic are really classes found in the System.Web.UI.WebControls namespace. Thus, it is possible to create your own specialized versions of these controls by writing classes that extend the base classes in the BCL. By doing so, you can override the default behavior of a control where desired and inherit the functionality with which you are satisfied. For example, if you are dissatisfied with the way the Calendar control renders on a particular browser (e.g., Netscape 6), you can write your own custom Calendar that provides its own implementation for Netscape but falls back to the default behavior for other browsers.

EXAMPLE

In this example, we will create a more complex J# ASP.NET application to demonstrate some of the many features discussed in this chapter. For this example, we're going to design a "Pop Quiz" Web Application that will test users on a few features of ASP.NET and then give them a score. Just to make things more interesting, we will also ask users to provide their names and birthdays (for the record, of course). Because this example is somewhat involved, it has been divided into numbered steps that you can follow. Complete source code for the entire example application can be found at o╌╍╌ JS050017.

Setting Up the Project (Quiz.aspx)

1. Open Visual Studio .NET and select **New Project.** Choose to create a new J# ASP.NET Web Application. Name it PopQuiz, but don't forget to leave localhost in the address, because we'll be running this application on our local machine. Click **OK,** and Visual Studio .NET will generate the appropriate code and open your new application to the design view.

2. Since we're creating a more professional-looking application, it won't do to keep the name WebForm1.aspx for the initial page

of the application. Right-click on `WebForm1.aspx` in the Solution Explorer and select **Rename.** Call it `Quiz.aspx`.

3. The Properties browser should currently be displaying the properties for `Quiz.aspx`. Change the `Title` property to something more appropriate, such as "J# ASP.NET Pop Quiz."

Designing the GUI

4. Drag and drop components into the Design window until it looks something like Figure 5.13. Don't worry if your controls don't look exactly like the ones in Figure 5.13 right away. We'll go over specific property changes in the next step.

5. We changed the font styles on most of the controls to make them look more attractive. Specifically, we changed the font name for every control to Arial, and we changed the sizes of the headings and made them bold. You can make these changes if you like, although it is not really necessary to the functionality of the application. There are, however, four specific property changes you need to make in order for the application to work:

  a. Change the `ID` properties of three of the items so that they are easier to refer to from the code. We called the first textbox "NameBox," the second "AgeBox," and the calendar control "BirthdayCalendar."

  b. Change the `VisibleDate` property of `BirthdayCalendar` to `1/1/1982` (or any other reasonable date).

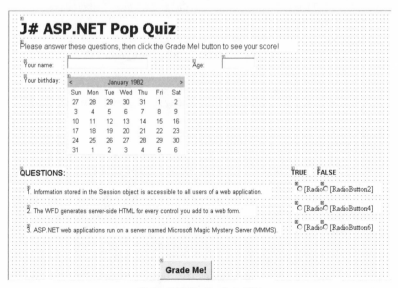

Figure 5.13 The PopQuiz GUI

This will be the starting date for your calendar. Remember that the users will be selecting their dates of birth and won't want to have to scroll backward or forward too many years to find them, so you should choose something close to your users' age group.

c. Change the ReadOnly property of AgeBox to True. We don't want users to be able to edit their ages directly. Instead, we want to generate the values in this box based on what users select on the BirthdayCalendar.

d. We need to organize the RadioButton objects into groups so that each true/false pair can have only one button selected at a time. Find the GroupName property for each RadioButton control. RadioButton 1 and 2 should be in a group named "1"; 3 and 4 should be in group "2"; 5 and 6 should be in group "3."

Adding Code to the GUI

6. Double-click on BirthdayCalendar and add the code in Listing 5.23 to the SelectionChanged() event handler method. You can ignore the odd line breaks in this listing.

```
private void BirthdayCalendar_SelectionChanged (Object sender,
  System.EventArgs e)
{
  System.DateTime today = BirthdayCalendar.get_TodaysDate();
  System.DateTime birthday =
    BirthdayCalendar.get_SelectedDate();
  int age = today.get_Year() - birthday.get_Year();

  // note: following check doesn't account for leap years
  if (today.get_DayOfYear() < birthday.get_DayOfYear())
    age--;
  AgeBox.set_Text(String.valueOf(age));
}
```

Listing 5.23 BirthdayCalendar_SelectionChanged() method

The code in Listing 5.23 finds the difference between the current day and the user's birthday, determines his or her age, and then puts that age in AgeBox. Note how the accessor methods get_TodaysDate() and get_SelectedDate() are used to access dates from a calendar.

7. Double-click on the **Grade Me!** button to open its Click()

event handler. This will be our Submit button for the form. Add the code in Listing 5.24 to the Button1_Click() method.

```
private void Button1_Click (Object sender, System.EventArgs e)
{
 get_Session().Add("name", NameBox.get_Text());
 get_Session().Add("age", AgeBox.get_Text());

 int score = 0;

 if (RadioButton2.get_Checked())
   score++;
 if (RadioButton3.get_Checked())
 score++;
 if (RadioButton6.get_Checked())
   score++;
 get_Session().Add("score",new Integer(score));
 get_Server().Transfer("Grade.aspx");
}
```

Listing 5.24 Button1_Click() method

The code in Listing 5.24 is responsible for adding the user's name, age, and score on the quiz to the session. Recall that the session is a user-specific object that can store items you want to be accessible throughout a user's visit to your application. We calculate the user's score by checking each correct answer to see whether it has been selected and adding 1 to the score if it has.

Finally, we use the Server.Transfer() method to forward the user to a new page named Grade.aspx, which is where the results of this quiz will be displayed. This method takes our existing HTTP request and hands it off to a new page rather than generating an HTTP response. The response will be generated by Grade.aspx, instead of Quiz.aspx.

Displaying the Grade (Grade.aspx)

8. The next step is to create a second page to display the user's grade. Right-click on **PopQuiz** in the Solution Explorer and select **Add → Add New Item.** Select a Web Form template and name it Grade.aspx, then click **OK.** A new file named Grade.aspx will be added to the solution. Double-click on Grade.aspx in the Solution Explorer to open its design view.

9. Drag two labels and a button onto the form and configure their properties so that they look like Figure 5.14. You will need to change the Text properties for each control, and you can also change the font styles if you so desire.

10. Double-click the **See My Score!** button to open its Click() event handler. Add the code in Listing 5.25 to this method.

```
private void Button1_Click (Object sender, System.EventArgs e)
{
 Integer myScore = (Integer)get_Session().get_Item("score");
 Label2.set_Text("You scored a " + myScore + " on the quiz.");
 switch (myScore.intValue())
 {
 case 3:
   Label2.set_Text(Label2.get_Text() + " Excellent!");
   break;
 case 2:
   Label2.set_Text(Label2.get_Text() + " Not bad!");
   break;
 case 1:
   Label2.set_Text(Label2.get_Text() + " Try harder!");
   break;
 case 0:
   Label2.set_Text(Label2.get_Text() + " Yikes! " +
 "Read CodeNotes for J# again.");
   break;
 };
}
```

Listing 5.25 Button1_Click() *in* Grade.aspx

This code is responsible for retrieving the user's score from the session and then determining an appropriate message depending on the score (using the switch statement). Note that everything you extract from the session is a generic Object, so you

Figure 5.14 Grade.aspx *design*

need to cast it to the appropriate class when extracting it (In-teger, in our case).

11. Finally, scroll up in the code view until you locate the Page_Load() method. This method is run before the page is displayed in the browser and is generally used to prepare the page and set up any important global variables. Insert into Page_Load() the three lines in Listing 5.26.

```
private void Page_Load(Object sender, System.EventArgs e)
{
  String name = (String)get_Session().get_Item("name");
  String age = (String)get_Session().get_Item("age");
  Label1.set_Text("You've finished the quiz, " + name +
    ". Click the button to see if you got a good score for a " +
    age + " year old.");
}
```

Listing 5.26 Page_Load()

The code in Listing 5.26 simply extracts the name and age items from the session and then uses them to create a personalized message in Label1. Note that we could also have extracted these values from the Request object the first time the page was loaded; however, when we click the **See My Score!** button on the page, a new Request is generated and the information would be lost (and name and age would become null), so using Session is a better choice in this example.

The PopQuiz application is complete. Run it (by pressing **CTRL + F5**), and try entering your name and age and filling out the quiz. Then submit your results, and check your score. To see what your application *should* look like when complete, please see ᶜᴺᵍ JS050018.

HOW AND WHY

How Can I Validate Input on Web Forms?

Validating user input has always been a prime concern for developers, and the Web is no exception. Enterprise applications often confirm a user's credentials (age, e-mail, password, etc.) before granting him or her access to certain resources. The code for such operations can reside in one of two places: on the browser, in the form of client-side JavaScript or VBScript, or on the server, in whatever language/

technology the application is written in (ASP.NET/ASP, JSP, CGI, etc.).

ASP.NET's *validation controls* give you the best of both worlds: they can generate either client-side or server-side code, depending upon the browser's capabilities. Furthermore, ASP.NET validation controls don't require you to write any code. Instead, validation controls abstract common tasks, such as determining whether a control's value falls within a given range or whether a field contains a value. You can configure these tasks using simple property settings and let ASP.NET take care of the specific code. You can find more information on ASP.NET validation controls at ⟡JS050019.

SUMMARY

As you experiment with the different Web Controls, you will see that some are almost identical to basic HTML, whereas others provide significant value in terms of the amount of boilerplate functionality that is automatically coded for you. Web Controls, combined with drag-and-drop form generation, make ASP.NET a powerful platform for rapid application development. You don't have to spend the time on routine code (such as validating a textbox) because ASP.NET will take care of it for you. Simply adjust a few settings and the necessary HTML and JavaScript will automatically appear.

This topic introduced a lot of Web Controls very briefly. For detailed instructions on how to use specific controls, the best place to look is always the MSDN (located on your local machine or at http://msdn.microsoft.com).

Chapter Summary

When designing J# Web Applications using ASP.NET, Visual Studio .NET's Web Forms Designer can almost make you forget that you are designing Web Applications at all. You can simply think of Web Application design with ASP.NET as being identical to Windows desktop application design, except that the output is going to a different place (a user's Web browser instead of a user's desktop).

When you drag Web Controls into the Design window, the WFD automatically generates server-side HTML code to represent the controls. This HTML code is specific to ASP.NET, and if you are taking advantage of VS .NET's full suite of Web development tools, you will rarely need to look at HTML, let alone edit it manually. Instead of adding control functionality directly to the HTML, ASP.NET Web Forms are linked to CodeBehind files, which contain all the initialization and event handler code for the Web Form and every control in it. You should include any code you want to execute when a Web Control is activated in the Code-Behind file. If your code affects how the Web Form will appear in a user's browser (e.g., you change the appearance of a control), ASP.NET will automatically generate the client-side HTML or JavaScript for you—you simply continue to use the BCL classes you learned about in Chapters 3 and 4 of this book.

For more detailed information on designing and deploying Web Applications with ASP.NET, we recommend *CodeNotes for ASP.NET.*

Chapter 6

—

WEB SERVICES

Web Services, to put it simply, allow an application running on one machine (written in any language) to call methods running on another machine (also written in any language) over the World Wide Web. The term *Web Services* actually refers to a large collection of protocols that have been implemented, in whole or in part, by many different platforms and languages in the form of application program interfaces (APIs). APIs are language-specific implementations of a protocol. Many Web Service protocols such as SOAP and the Web Service Description Language (WSDL), are defined by an independent body called the World Wide Web Consortium (www.w3.org). The W3C has developed and maintains many of the standards used by .NET Web Services to enable seamless communication between Web Service methods and client applications over the Web.

So how does this "magical" communication between two applications—possibly written in entirely different languages, development environments, or operating systems—happen? Basically, Web Services and clients use the previously mentioned APIs in order to transform language-specific code (e.g., J# data types) into a *language-independent* medium. Specifically, a Web Service written in any language must be able to use an API called SOAP (formerly an acronym for Simple Object Access Protocol) to translate its own data types into SOAP data types. Most common data types (integers, strings, floats) have SOAP equivalents. In addition, the SOAP grammar can also be used to describe objects (i.e., user-created, arbitrary data types). Any language that supports the SOAP API and knows how to translate its own data types into SOAP can be used to write and consume Web Services. A typical scenario might be as follows:

1. A Web Service client knows about a Web Service that has a method the client wants to call. (The client knows how to call methods by means of a WSDL contract published by the Web Service creator. We'll look at these contracts subsequently.)
2. The client creates a SOAP message that contains a request for the Web Service method that it wants to call. Any parameters required by the Web Service method are provided by the client, who translates them from the client language data types into SOAP data types.
3. The SOAP message (called a *SOAP request*) is transported across the Web by piggybacking on an HTTP POST request. Recall that we discussed HTTP GET and POST requests in Chapter 5.
4. The target Web Service receives the SOAP message and translates the SOAP method call and parameters into its own language (using its own implementation of the SOAP API). The Web Service method executes with the provided parameters and generates a return value. Remember, the client might use a totally different language (e.g., Perl) than the Web Service (e.g., J#). Because both sides understand SOAP, the communication can still flow.
5. The Web Service produces its own SOAP message (a *SOAP response*), which includes the return value it just generated (translated into a SOAP data type, of course). This message is sent back to the client, again piggybacking on an HTTP message.
6. The client receives the SOAP message and translates the returned value from SOAP into its own data type. It then continues running, using the returned value just as if it had been generated locally.

In order to facilitate the sending of messages back and forth, a typical Web Service involves three distinct components. First, you need a *contract* that defines the service. Second, you need a *producer,* or host, for the service. Finally, you need a *consumer,* or client, to use (consume) the service.

• **Contract** The Web Service contract defines the name of the service, the service's input and output parameters, and the method of communication with the service. The contract is always an XML document that follows a rigidly defined XML

Schema (we will discuss both XML and XML Schema in the "Core Concepts" section of this chapter). The contract does not specify which software you must use for either the server or the client—it is a language-neutral document that any Web-Service-capable programming language must know how to read. In J# Web Services, as with most Web Services, the contract takes the form of a WSDL document. WSDL will be explained in further detail in the "Core Concepts" section.

- **Producer** The producer generates the Web Service and hosts it. In J#, the producer is a combination of Visual Studio .NET (in which the Web Service is designed) and Internet Information Services (IIS; the Web server used to host .NET Web Services). The real power of Web Services is that the contract isolates the producer from the client, meaning that even though the Web Service is designed in J# and hosted by IIS, the Web Service client can be written in an entirely different language and running on a different machine.

- **Consumer** The consumer, or client, finds the appropriate contract, connects to the producer, and uses the Web Service. A J# Web Service client can be any kind of .NET application (console, Windows, etc.). You simply add a special kind of reference called a *Web Reference* to your application, and your program will be able to call methods on a Web Service as though it were part of the project. A client does *not* have to be written in the same language as the Web Service; however, for the purposes of this CodeNotes we will write both clients and services in J#.

This chapter will provide you with a basic introduction to writing Web Services and clients in J#. You will learn how to write Web Service methods and how to create clients that can call and utilize these methods over the Web.

Simple Application

Designing a J# Web Service using the Visual Studio .NET IDE is actually similar to developing a class library (as we did in Chapter 3). You write classes and methods, but you don't write a main() method, because the classes you create will actually be deployed as Web Services and called by a separate client application via the Web. You never need to interact directly with SOAP, WSDL, or any other Web protocol, as they are all handled behind the scenes by the ASP.NET engine. You don't even have to learn any new coding techniques. All you need to do is add special *attributes* to your classes and methods (which we will demonstrate in a moment), in order to indicate that they should be available over the Web, and Visual Studio .NET will do the rest.

In this simple application we will create a "hello world" Web Service in the simplest possible manner, which will demonstrate just how easy writing J# Web Services and Web Service clients can be. As with the ASP.NET applications discussed in Chapter 5, you will need a copy of IIS installed on your machine in order to run the Web Service provider examples in this chapter. However, you can run the client code without IIS.

HelloService

We start by creating a new J# ASP.NET Web Service named HelloService. You can find the complete code for this Web Service at ᴼᴺⓎ JS060001.

Getting Started: The Web Service Template

Open Visual Studio .NET and select **New Project.** Choose the **ASP.NET Web Service** template from the J# Projects folder. Name your project by editing the URL in the **Location** field. Leave the http://localhost/ part of the URL and change the default service name (WebService1) to HelloService. Click the **OK** button to have Visual Studio .NET create your new Web Service project.

As with the other Visual Studio .NET templates you have used in previous chapters, the Web Service template contains a significant amount of pregenerated code. The files that are automatically included in the project are very similar to those found in an ASP.NET Web Application project. You can find more details on these files in Chapter 5. In fact, the only immediately apparent difference between an ASP.NET Web Application and an ASP.NET Web Service is that the default file (the one that VS .NET creates and opens when you first create a project) is named Service1.asmx instead of WebForm1.aspx, as shown in Figure 6.1. Because a Web Service is designed to be accessed by other applications and not directly by users, it does not use forms of any kind.

Click the "click here to switch to code view" link shown in Figure 6.1. This will open a file named Service1.asmx.jsl, the CodeBehind for the Web Service.

Building the Service

Listing 6.1 shows the code for Service1.asmx.jsl. Notice that Visual Studio .NET has automatically generated not only the necessary support code (import statements, a Web Service class, etc.), but also a default HelloWorld() Web Service method (highlighted in bold).

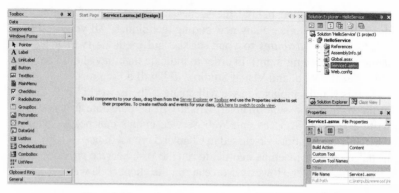

*Figure 6.1 A new Web Service project (*HelloService*)*

```
package HelloService;

import System.* ;
import System.Collections.*;
import System.ComponentModel.*;
import System.Data.*;
import System.Diagnostics.*;
import System.Web.*;
import System.Web.Services.*;

/**
 * Summary description for Service1.
 */
public class Service1 extends System.Web.Services.WebService
{
 public Service1()
 {
  //CODEGEN: This call is required by the ASP.NET
//Web Services Designer
  InitializeComponent();
 }

 #region Component Designer generated code
 // generated code removed from example for brevity

 /**
  * WEB SERVICE EXAMPLE
```

```
 * The HelloWorld() example service returns the string Hello
 * World. To build, uncomment the following lines then save
 * and build the project. To test this Web service, press F5
 */
// /** @attribute WebMethod() */
// public String HelloWorld()
// {
// return "Hello World";
// }
}
```

Listing 6.1 Web Service with hello() *method*

Normally, you would delete HelloWorld() before starting to write your Web Service (HelloWorld() is a sample Web Service function included in all Web Service templates). But because we are only creating a simple application, we will actually use HelloWorld() to demonstrate a simple Web Service. All you need to do is erase the "//" comment characters from the beginning of each of the five lines of the HelloWorld() method. Don't worry about the actual code in Service1.asmx.jsl just yet—we'll look at attributes, Web Service classes, and Web Service methods in much more detail throughout the rest of this chapter. For now, understand that the HelloWorld() method is a normal method that takes no parameters and returns a String that reads "Hello World". Note that we removed a large chunk of the template from Listing 6.1 in order to maintain the brevity of this example. The removed code, which is normally hidden from view, was generated by VS .NET's Component Designer and should not be modified manually. You can find more details concerning what appears inside the hidden region in the "Windows Forms Example" section in Chapter 4.

Deploying the Service
We can deploy HelloService() simply by building the application (press **Ctrl + Shift + B**). Most of the files necessary for the Web Service were added to the project automatically when it was first created. Building the application will generate additional files for use with the Web Service, including a WSDL contract. Recall that the WSDL contract is an XML document that describes the methods available in a Web Service, as well as the procedure for accessing those methods. In .NET, WSDL contracts are created automatically for any Web Service, and you will never have to edit WSDL code manually. Once you build and deploy a Web Service for the first time, it will remain deployed even after Visual Studio .NET is no longer running. Each time you build a Web

Service you are actually redeploying your new version over the currently deployed version (unless you change the build location or move the original build).

HelloClient

Now that we have a working Web Service, we can create a client to invoke it. We could write a Web Service client in any language, and as long as it had access to the Web it could use our Web Service (thanks to the fact that Web Services and clients use SOAP as a universal standard for communicating between them). For this simple application, our client is simply a normal Windows application. It does not include any Web-Service-specific tags (such as the /** @attribute WebMethod() */ line from Listing 6.1). Instead, we add what is called a *Web Reference* to HelloService. A Web Reference is similar to the normal references we saw in Chapters 3 and 4 of this CodeNotes, except that, rather than referencing an assembly, our Web Reference links to a WSDL contract that describes an existing Web Service. Visual Studio .NET examines the WSDL document and creates a proxy class representing the Web Service. A *proxy class* can be instantiated just like any other class and contains all the methods available on the Web Service. You can call these methods as though they were normal methods; however, underneath the hood, the methods in the proxy class are actually constructing SOAP messages and communicating with the Web Service over HTTP. Visual Studio .NET hides all of this underlying code from you, and all you need to do is call methods on the proxy class.

Start by selecting **New → Project** from the VS .NET File menu. Select the Visual J# Windows Application template and name your new application HelloClient. Click **OK,** and Visual Studio .NET will generate a new Windows application project for you with a default form named Form1.jsl. (If you don't remember how to work with Windows applications, please go back and reread Chapter 4 of this CodeNotes before continuing.)

Drag a Button and a Label onto Form1.jsl so that it looks like Figure 6.2. Note that you can make your button and label look like the ones in Figure 6.2 by using the Properties browser to edit their Text properties.

We will now add a Web Reference to HelloService. Select **Add Web Reference** from the Project menu. Type the address of your Web Service file into the URL field (this address should be http://localhost/HelloService/Service1.asmx) and then click the **Go** button. Visual Studio .NET will locate your Web Service and display some information about it in the main area of the Add Web Reference screen, as shown in Figure 6.3.

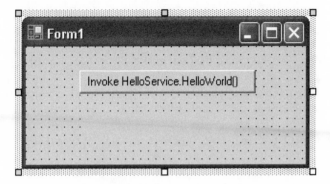

Figure 6.2 Form for a Web Service client

Click the **Add Reference** button in order to add a Web reference to HelloService to your client application. As mentioned previously, when you add a Web Reference, Visual Studio .NET generates a special class called a proxy class to represent the Web Service in your client application. Notice that a new section called Web References has been added to your Solution Explorer and that there is an item under Web References named localhost. Visual Studio .NET uses the URL of the Web Service

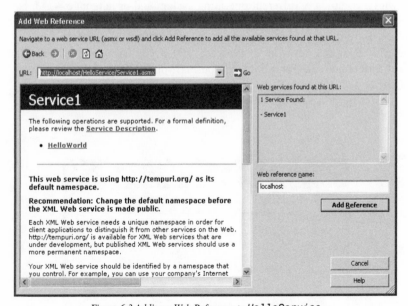

Figure 6.3 Adding a Web Reference to HelloService

as the name of the proxy class, which is `localhost` in this case. We'll show you how to change this name to something more meaningful later in this chapter.

Finally, we need to add the code that calls the `HelloWorld()` method in `HelloService`. We're going to add this code to the `Click` handler of our button, so double-click the button to open the code editor. Add the bold code in Listing 6.2 to `button1_Click()`.

```
private void button1_Click (Object sender, System.EventArgs e)
{
  localhost.Service1 myHelloService = new localhost.Service1();
  label1.set_Text(myHelloService.HelloWorld());
}
```

Listing 6.2 Client code to invoke `HelloService`

Build and run `HelloClient` by pressing **CTRL + F5,** then click on the button. The text of the label should change to read "Hello World," as shown in Figure 6.4. Again, you can download the source code for this simple application at ⚛JS060001.

We built this Web Service and consumed it on our local machine, but the steps would have been identical had we decided to consume a Web Service that was running on the other side of the world and was written with a completely different operating system and/or language—as long as it conformed to the XML Web Service standards. For those who are new to remote computing concepts such as this, it may seem as if this level of integration is to be expected. But if you have ever tried to use other technologies for remote computing, you will appreciate the convenience of XML Web Services and the fact that the .NET Framework natively supports both consumption and creation.

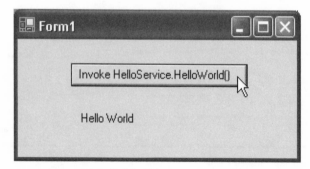

Figure 6.4 The `HelloClient` *application in action*

CORE CONCEPTS

Some Brief Definitions

Before getting into the actual technologies involved in Web Services, it is important that you understand some basic terms and their definitions. The technologies in the following list, although not directly related to Web Services, provide the basis from which many Web Service technologies are derived.

- **XML** Extensible Markup Language (XML) is a simple markup language for representing structured, text-based data. If you are familiar with HTML (which is also a markup language), you can think of XML as being similar to HTML, except that XML tags have no fixed meaning. XML does not specifically define <title>, <body>, or <p> tags. Instead, the creators of an XML document can define their own tags to fit the data being represented. A simple XML document looks like Listing 6.3.

```
<?xml version="1.0"?>
<authors>
 <author>
  <name>Craig Wills</name>
 </author>
 <author>
  <name>Rob McGovern</name>
 </author>
</authors>
```

Listing 6.3 A simple XML document

For a more thorough introduction to XML, please see ᴄɴJS060002 or *CodeNotes for XML*.

- **Grammar** An XML grammar is a defined set of XML tags targeted at a specific industry. XML grammars typically *do* have tags with fixed meanings, and these meanings are defined by a special document called an XML Schema (which we will discuss in a moment). Some common XML grammars include SVG (an XML grammar for storing vector graphics in text format), ebXML (an XML grammar for describing electronic businesses), and SOAP (an XML grammar for transmitting object data over the Web). SOAP is the primary protocol used by J# Web Services, and we will cover it in much more detail later in its own "Core Concept" section.

• **XML Schema**   You can think of XML Schema as an XML meta grammar. XML Schema is actually an XML grammar for defining XML grammars. Using XML Schema, you can define which elements are allowed in an XML document, and the combinations and order in which those elements can occur. The following is an XML Schema that defines a grammar that could be used for the XML document in Listing 6.3.

```
<?xml version="1.0"?>
<xsd:schema xmlns:xsd="http://www.w3.org/2001/XMLSchema"
      targetNameSpace="http://www.codenotes.com"
      xmlns="http://www.codenotes.com"
      elementFormDefault="qualified">
 <xsd:element name="authors">
  <xsd:complexType>
   <xsd:sequence>
    <xsd:element name="author" maxOccurs="unbounded">
     <xsd:sequence>
      <xsd:complexType>
       <xsd:element name="name" type="xsd:string"/>
      </xsd:complexType>
     </xsd:sequence>
    </xsd:element>
   </xsd:sequence>
  </xsd:complexType>
 </xsd:element>
</xsd:schema>
```

Listing 6.4 A simple XML Schema

XML Schema may seem complicated, and it is. But all you really need to know for the purposes of this chapter is that the data types used in SOAP messages are defined using XML Schema, and that J# Web Services transform your data types and classes into XML Schema types behind the scenes in order to transport them from Web Service to client and back again. For a more thorough introduction to XML Schema, please see ⊶JS060003 or *CodeNotes for XML*.

SOAP

Formerly, SOAP was an acronym for the Simple Object Access Protocol. As of the most recent release from the W3C, however, the name "SOAP" simply refers to the API rather than to the components of an acronym. Regardless, SOAP is an XML grammar used to send messages between clients and Web Services. SOAP has emerged as the standard for remote procedure calling due to industry support from major vendors such as Microsoft and IBM. Web Service consumers and producers use SOAP messages to transmit data. In ASP.NET, the generation of SOAP messages is done entirely behind the scenes, so you will never have to work with SOAP directly. Nevertheless, it is helpful to take a closer look at SOAP in order to learn more about the manner in which your data is being transported between Web Services and clients.

SOAP messages are usually transported as the payload of an HTTP POST message. Often referred to as a SOAP *envelope,* a SOAP message contains XML-encoded data (which, of course, is simply text) and acts as an intermediary format between a Web Service and its client(s). Both clients and servers must leverage an implementation of the SOAP specification. This implementation is responsible for creating and interpreting SOAP messages and mapping the SOAP data types into language-specific data type structures. For example, a J# client must know how to encode a .NET String object into a SOAP string, as well as how to extract the information from a SOAP string back into a .NET String, without the inclusion of any language-specific instructions in the SOAP message itself. The SOAP specification uses XML Schema as its data typing mechanism, and therefore implementations must also leverage an XML parser that understands XML Schemas.

In our simple application, HelloClient sent the HTTP POST request in Listing 6.5 containing a SOAP message to HelloService.

```
POST /HelloService/Service1.asmx HTTP/1.1
Host: localhost
Content-Type: text/xml; charset=utf-8
Content-Length: length
SOAPAction: "http://tempuri.org/HelloWorld"

<?xml version="1.0" encoding="utf-8"?>
<soap:Envelope xmlns:xsi="http://www.w3.org/2001/XMLSchema-
instance" xmlns:xsd="http://www.w3.org/2001/XMLSchema"
xmlns:soap="http://schemas.xmlsoap.org/soap/envelope/">
  <soap:Body>
   <HelloWorld xmlns="http://tempuri.org/" />
  </soap:Body>
</soap:Envelope>
```

Listing 6.5 A SOAP response message from HelloClient *to* HelloService

Note from Listing 6.5 that HTTP POST requests containing SOAP messages require a special header named SOAPAction. This attribute contains a *namespace* that is used by ASP.NET to represent the location of a Web Service (tempuri.org is the default namespace for all new Web Services). Web Service namespaces are simply arbitrary strings that don't have to correspond to a real URL. The reason most Web Service designers use URLs for namespaces is that a URL is guaranteed to be unique, provided the designers or their company own that URL. You will find more about assigning namespaces to your Web Services in the "Creating J# Web Services" section of this chapter.

In response to the SOAP request message in Listing 6.5, Hello-Service would send the HTTP SOAP response message in Listing 6.6 back to HelloClient.

```
HTTP/1.1 200 OK
Content-Type: text/xml; charset=utf-8
Content-Length: length

<?xml version="1.0" encoding="utf-8"?>
<soap:Envelope xmlns:xsi="http://www.w3.org/2001/XMLSchema-
instance" xmlns:xsd="http://www.w3.org/2001/XMLSchema"
xmlns:soap="http://schemas.xmlsoap.org/soap/envelope/">
 <soap:Body>
  <HelloWorldResponse xmlns="http://tempuri.org/">
   <HelloWorldResult>Hello World</HelloWorldResult>
  </HelloWorldResponse>
 </soap:Body>
</soap:Envelope>
```

Listing 6.6 A SOAP response message from HelloService *to* HelloClient

As you can see from Listings 6.5 and 6.6, the ASP.NET engine transforms .NET class names, method names, and variable names into elements in SOAP messages. This process is called *serialization*. The reverse process, the translating of SOAP elements into .NET data types, is called *deserialization*.

Because you will never have to work with SOAP directly when creating Web Services with the .NET Framework, the details of the SOAP grammar and of the manner in which Web Services serialize and deserialize SOAP messages are beyond the scope of this book. If you are interested in learning more about SOAP, please see *CodeNotes for Web Services in Java and .NET.*

WSDL

Web Services Description Language (WSDL) is an XML grammar for describing the methods available in a Web Service and the procedure by which a client should invoke the methods. A WSDL document is often referred to as a *contract* between a Web Service and its clients. The Web Service agrees to process a request and provide a return value for any SOAP message formatted as specified by the WSDL document. The client, upon reading this contract, knows the kinds of message that the service wants and can be programmed to send messages in the correct formats.

In addition to informing clients about the methods that are available, WSDL documents also provide other information, such as what the data type parameters should be (including XML Schema code for complex types, if necessary), where the service is located, and what namespaces should be used for the various components of the SOAP request. In this way, clients can interface with Web Services without having to look at the code or underlying structure of the service itself.

Fortunately, WSDL files are created automatically by ASP.NET. WSDL is generated automatically when the service is deployed, and the WSDL contract can be accessed by any client application in order to determine how it should interact with the service. Because you will never have to work with WSDL directly, the elements of the WSDL grammar itself are beyond the scope of this CodeNotes. For a thorough tutorial on WSDL and how it is generated in .NET Web Services, please see *Code-Notes for Web Services in Java and .NET.*

Deploying Web Services

An ASP.NET Web Service consists of a special type of `.aspx` page running under IIS. The ASP.NET engine knows that a request for the page is actually a Web Service (thanks to SOAP), and handles the request appropriately. VS .NET does all the work of deploying Web Services under the hood. All you need to do in order to deploy a Web Service is compile the Web Service project (by pressing **CTRL + SHIFT + B** or selecting **Build Project** from the Build menu). All the necessary files are generated automatically for your Web Service, either when you first create the project or in the build process. Your Web Service is deployed to the directory that you indicated when you first created the project. This directory could be in the default virtual directory or in a virtual directory you created (Web Services, like ASP.NET applications, are hosted in IIS virtual directories). If you want to deploy a Web Service to another machine, VS .NET also allows you to create an install package (an .MSI file) that can then be run on the other machine in order to create all the necessary directories automatically (see ☜JS030014).

Wherever you decide to save the service, the directory structure in which the files are stored will look something like Figure 6.5.

Once you have compiled and deployed a Web Service, it will be ac-

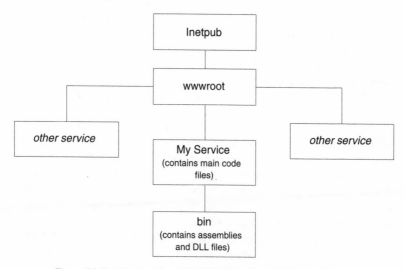

Figure 6.5 The directory structure of a Web Service created with VS .NET

cessible via a Web Service client or a Web browser. For example, suppose we have created a virtual directory for Web Services called cn_services, and we have deployed a service called myService on http:// www.codenotes.com. Clients or Web browsers could then access this Web Service at http://www.codenotes.com/cn_services/myService.asmx. Alternatively, if we were working on the host computer for www.codenotes. com (that is, the machine on which the website is actually running), we could access the same service using the address http://localhost/cn_ services/myService.asmx. Throughout this book, we will always access the example services via localhost.

Testing Web Services
ASP.NET provides a special Web interface for Web Services. The Web interface can be accessed by pointing a Web browser to the address of a Web Service you have created (e.g., http://localhost/HelloService/ Service1.asmx). The Web interface has two primary functions:

- It includes "help pages" that provide some information on problems that might occur with your Web Service. For example, one of these pages will often warn you if the namespace you are using for your Web Service is one that might cause conflicts with other services. In addition, the help pages will show you how SOAP (and other) messages to and from your service must be structured.

• It includes a Web Service testing tool that allows you to enter parameters in a form, click a button in order to invoke the service, and then view the response. Web Services, after all, can be accessed from any type of client. ASP.NET provides a simple HTML-based client that can be used as a test platform in order to ensure that your service is behaving properly.

To load the Web Service created in the "Simple Application" section of this chapter, type http://localhost/HelloService/Service1.asmx into the address bar in Internet Explorer. You will see a Web page like the one in Figure 6.6.

Clicking on **Service Description** will display the WSDL contract for this Web Service. Clicking on the name of a method (for example, HelloWorld) will open a new page with a form that allows you to invoke the selected method. The test page also has a list of formatted messages demonstrating the manner in which SOAP requests to this method should be constructed, as well as what the SOAP response messages to each of these calls will look like. The page for the HelloWorld method is shown in Figure 6.7.

You can click the **Invoke** button in order to try out the HelloWorld Web Method and view the results (as XML). If HelloWorld required parameters, you would be able to type values for these parameters in the fields before clicking **Invoke.** Note that the test operation implemented by this Web interface uses an HTTP GET call to the service and does not send (or receive) SOAP messages. Even so, the Web interface can be a very useful utility for testing whether the correct data is being received and sent by your service, as well as whether it functions as expected.

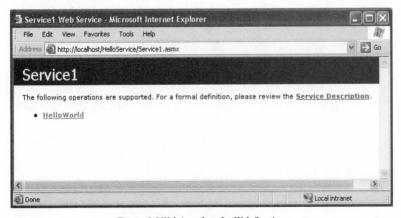

Figure 6.6 Web interface for Web Services

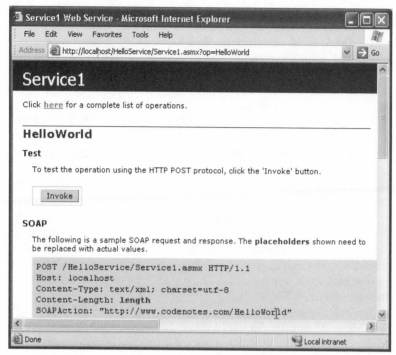

Figure 6.7 Test invoker and message descriptions for the `HelloWorld( )` *method*

Topic: Creating J# Web Services

This chapter is divided into two topics. In this first topic, we will examine the process of creating a J# Web Service project, writing Web Service code, and deploying the Web Service using IIS. We will also look at how you can customize your Web Services so that they can be invoked by clients written in languages other than those supported by .NET (such as Java).

In the second topic, we will demonstrate how you can write Web Service client applications quickly and easily in J#. You will discover that any kind of .NET project (Windows application, console application, ASP.NET Web Application) can easily leverage existing Web Services.

CORE CONCEPTS

Creating Web Services
Creating a Web Service in Visual Studio .NET is as easy as creating a standard Windows application, Web Application, or any other application. All you need to do is create a new J# Web Service project:

1. To begin, open Visual Studio .NET and select **New Project.**
2. Select the J# ASP.NET Web Service template.
3. Change the location of your Web Service to something meaningful (other than the default, http://localhost/WebService1) before clicking **OK,** because it will be difficult to change the name
   later. Because you are developing Web Services on your local
   machine, you should leave the http://localhost/ part of the address as is.
4. Click **OK.** Visual Studio .NET will generate a new J# Web Service project for you.

Once you have created a new project using the template, you can
quickly move on to writing your Web Service code.

The .NET Web Service Template

Most of the Web-Service-related work in .NET Web Services is done
under the hood, saving you the trouble of coding a lot of boilerplate material. Your job as a developer is made even easier by the templates generated by VS .NET for J# Web Services. These templates include
virtually all the code needed to deploy a Web Service successfully, including special Web-Service-specific attributes such as WebService and
WebMethod (which will be explained later in this topic). All you need to
do is add functionality; that is, you need to specify what your Web Service does and what value it should return.

The template generated by Visual Studio .NET for J# Web Services is
shown in Listing 6.7 (some formatting has been added for readability).

```
package SampleService;

import System.* ;
import System.Collections.*;
import System.ComponentModel.*;
import System.Data.*;
import System.Diagnostics.*;
import System.Web.*;
import System.Web.Services.*;

/**
 * Summary description for Service1.
 */
public class Service1 extends System.Web.Services.WebService
{
  public Service1()
```

```
{
 //CODEGEN: This call is required by the ASP.NET Web
 //     Services Designer
 InitializeComponent();
}

#region Component Designer generated code

// generated region code removed for brevity

#endregion

/**

 * WEB SERVICE EXAMPLE

 * The HelloWorld() example service returns the string Hello

 * World. To build, uncomment the following lines then save

 * and build the project. To test this Web service, press F5

 */

// /** @attribute WebMethod() */
// public String HelloWorld()
// {
// return "Hello World";
// }
}
```

Listing 6.7 J# Web Service template

The parts of the code that you will need to manipulate are highlighted in bold. The "Component Designer generated code" region will be hidden from view unless you choose to expand it, and it is either generated boilerplate or code that should be modified only by the Web Services Designer application.

The Web Services Designer

When you create a Web Service in Visual Studio .NET, your view of the service will begin on the Web Services Designer screen. The Web Services Designer screen allows you to add Visual Studio components (such as database connections) to your Web Service class by dragging them into the Design window from the toolbox at the left of the Visual Studio screen. When you add a component, you can modify it by editing its properties (in the Properties browser, usually located at the bottom right of the Visual Studio window). The Web Services Designer will automatically add and modify the code that controls these components. Code generated by the Web Services Designer should not be modified by means of the code editor.

Though most of the components that can be added by using the Web Services Designer are beyond the scope of this CodeNotes, you can find an example of a Web Service designed by using the Web Services Designer at °CN⟩JS030004.

The remainder of this topic will focus on modifying code by using the code editor in order to get the results you want from a Web Service.

The WebMethod Attribute

If you look at the bold code in Listing 6.7, you may notice the (somewhat odd-looking) line directly before the HelloWorld() method declaration shown in Listing 6.8.

```
/** @attribute WebMethod() */
```

Listing 6.8 A J# attribute

The line in Listing 6.8 declares a J# attribute. An *attribute* is a nonprogrammatic statement (i.e., not J#) that influences code generation. Attributes are sometimes referred to as *metadata,* which means that although attributes are not part of the actual code, they can influence the manner in which that code is transformed from J# into an MSIL assembly. Attributes are used throughout the .NET Framework to indicate specific locations where code must be treated in a special way. In the case of Web Services, attributes are used to indicate when methods (or classes, as we will see in the next section) are Web-Service-related and must therefore be made available over the Web. Without the attribute in Listing 6.8, our HelloWorld() method in Listing 6.7 would not be accessible as a Web Service, and our project would become a simple ASP.NET page rather than a Web Service.

Every method that you want to be available to Web Service clients must begin with a WebMethod attribute. You can have as many methods with WebMethod attributes as you want in a Web Service class, but methods that do not begin with WebMethod will not be available on the Web. Note that private methods cannot be Web Methods.

An attribute can also have parameters. Parameters are usually optional and are used to indicate that certain aspects of a Web Method should be something other than the default. For example, you might use a parameter to indicate that a Web Service should exist in a specific namespace (remember that every Web Service must be located in a namespace so that a client application can find it).

The WebMethod attribute has a collection of parameters that can be used to modify various aspects of the Web Service. Some of these are as follows:

- CacheDuration   Allows you to indicate how long a method response should be cached in memory. The attribute's value should be an integer representing a length of time in seconds. By default, responses will not be cached (that is, CacheDuration=0). You might want to use this parameter if the response from your method changes frequently, to ensure users always get up-to-date responses.
- Description   The value of this property will appear on the ASP.NET Web interface (discussed in the "Testing Web Services" core concept) for the method and in the WSDL file as a description of the operation. Remember that WSDL files are used to describe the methods and parameters of a Web Service to a client.
- EnableSession   You may remember from Chapter 5 that a user's session is a specific area of memory on the server dedicated to the particular user. By setting EnableSession to false, you can tell the server not to maintain session state (that is, it will not keep track of who accesses the method and when). By default, EnableSession is true. You might want to set Enable-Session to false if you want a stateless Web Service that does not need to remember a user's actions from one call to the next.
- MessageName   Allows you to overload methods of the same name by giving each version a unique message name (which will appear in the WSDL file and SOAP messages to and from the service). Simply repeating method names with different parameters (as you would normally do when overloading methods) is not enough for SOAP and may cause confusion when a client tries to access a particular method. You should always use MessageName to give your Web Service methods unique names when you have more than one method with the same name in the J# code, even if these methods have different parameters.

WebMethod parameters should be separated by commas when more than one occurs in a single WebMethod attribute. Listing 6.9 shows an example of a J# WebMethod using several parameters.

```
/** @attribute WebMethod(CacheDuration=120,
              MessageName="myMethod",
              Description="This is my Web method.")
*/
```

Listing 6.9 WebMethod *attribute example*

Note that when you try to format your attribute by putting parameters on multiple lines (as we did in Listing 6.9), VS .NET will automatically insert * characters at the beginning of each line (this is because J# attributes use a similar format to JavaDocs, which traditionally put * characters at the beginning of every line of comments). You will need to remove these characters manually, as the * character is not allowed inside parameter listings.

The WebService Attribute

Attributes can be applied to classes as well as to methods. The Web-Service attribute can be applied to any class that inherits from System.Web.Services.WebService. The WebService attribute indicates that a particular class will contain methods that will be exposed over the Web. WebService was not included in the template from Listing 6.7 because it is not actually necessary—methods inside a class can be exposed as Web Service methods, even if the class is not explicitly declared as a Web Service. However, if you want to supply any parameters that apply to the entire class, you will need to use a WebService attribute.

Like the WebMethod attribute, the WebService attribute allows you to provide a comma-separated list of parameters. Of particular note is the Namespace attribute, which allows you to provide a default namespace for all methods in the Web Service class. If you have created and run the simple application from the beginning of this chapter, you may have noticed that the ASP.NET Web Service interface warns that the Web Service is using http://tempuri.org/ as its default namespace. The Namespace attribute allows you to fix this problem by specifying a default namespace that will be more unique to your Web Services.

The WebService attribute actually supports three parameters:

- Namespace   Indicates the namespace in which this Web Service will exist. Clients will use this namespace to access the Web Service. You should use the Namespace attribute to change this namespace before publishing your Web Service, because the default one is used to represent all .NET services in progress and will not serve to identify your application uniquely. As a general rule, most developers build the namespace based on a Web address. For example, CodeNotes Web Services would generally use a namespace of http://www.codenotes.com.

- Name   Used to give your Web Service a specific name. By default, .NET Web Services are named after the file or class that contains the Web Service. Web Service names are used both as titles on the ASP.NET Web Service interface and as titles in the WSDL document.
- Description   Also displayed in the ASP.NET Web Service interface and included in the WSDL file. Description is basically a human-readable description of the Web Service that allows client writers to find out more about what your Web Service does. Description can contain any text you want to use to describe your service.

Listing 6.10 shows an example of a J# WebService attribute for a Web Service named myService.

```
/** @attribute
WebService(Namespace="http://www.codenotes.com",
  Name="myService",
  Description="This is a Web Service.")
*/
```

Listing 6.10 A WebService example

As mentioned previously, WebService is really an optional attribute, and you do not need to include it. When you use a Web Service template to create a Web Service, the processing directive that marks the project as a Web Service is stored in the file Global.asax. For any Web Service you intend to make public, however, it is a good idea to ensure that the WebService attribute is included.

Making Web Services Cross-Language Compatible

As we have seen thus far, most of the actual SOAP and HTTP work in ASP.NET is done under the hood. You can create and deploy Web Services without even knowing what SOAP is, provided you understand that the client applications that access your Web Service will also be written using any .NET language. However, one of the biggest advantages of Web Services is that the clients and services do not need to be written in the same language. However, each language must have its own version of the SOAP API. For example, .NET Web Services use an API written in MSIL to interact with Web Services, whereas Java Web

Services must use an API written in Java. And, although all SOAP APIs generate SOAP messages, at the time of this writing, there are definite differences between how .NET Web Services and Web Services in other languages (such as Java) generate, structure, and read SOAP messages. These differences often necessitate extra work in order for clients in one language to interact with services in another. If you are trying to make your Web Services as universally accessible as possible (as you should be), you will sometimes need to do a little extra work and customize aspects of your Web Services and clients in order to resolve compatibility issues.

In .NET Web Services, improving compatibility involves adding code in order to force certain components of a SOAP message to be included, even though .NET clients don't need them to function correctly. Specifically, .NET does not require that each parameter sent to or from a Web Service indicate its data type. .NET determines the data type of an element by looking at its content. Many other implementations of SOAP in other languages (such as Apache SOAP 2.2, a common Java SOAP API) cannot deserialize a SOAP message unless it is told exactly what data type each parameter contains. Therefore, we need to force outgoing SOAP messages from .NET Web Services (and clients as well, as we will see in the next topic) to include an XML Schema data type for each parameter. To do this we use the SoapRpcMethod attribute.

The SoapRpcMethod attribute is used *in addition to* the ordinary Web-Method attribute and indicates not only that the code that follows is a method that should be made available on this service, but also that this method should include XML Schema data types in its responses.

In order to use SoapRpcMethod, you must first add the import statement in Listing 6.11 to the top of your Web Service class file.

```
import System.Web.Services.Protocols.*;
```

Listing 6.11 Importing the Protocols namespace

The System.Web.Services.Protocols namespace includes classes for dealing with various formatting issues in SOAP and HTTP messages. The J# Web Services template does not import this namespace for you automatically.

SoapRpcMethod is used as shown in Listing 6.12.

```
/** @attribute WebMethod()
   @attribute
SoapRpcMethod(Action="http://www.codenotes.com/Rpc",
      RequestNamespace="http://www.codenotes.com/SUB",
      ResponseNamespace="http://www.codenotes.com/SUB"))
```

```
*/
public String HelloWorld()
{
 return "Hello World";
}
```

<hr>

Listing 6.12 SoapRpcMethod format

As you can see in Listing 6.12, the SoapRpcMethod attribute takes three parameters:

- Action   Dictates the value of the SoapAction header of a SOAP request accessing this method. All .NET Web Services require SoapAction headers to function correctly, and some implementations (such as Apache SOAP 2.2) require extra code to ensure that SoapAction is included.
- RequestNamespace   Provides a unique namespace for requests. Clients should use this namespace to target their requests at this method.
- ResponseNamespace   Provides a unique namespace for responses. Parameters returned to the client will be in this namespace.

.NET allows further customization of SOAP messages, including the use of literal encoding styles (see the "Design Notes" section later in this topic) and customization of the organization of parameters in the SOAP message. See CodeNotes pointer ⟲JS030004 for an example of some other SOAP message customization techniques.

EXAMPLE

Due to space constraints in this book, we have placed the example for this topic online. Please see ⟲JS060005 for an example of a relatively complex J# Web Service.

DESIGN NOTES

UDDI

UDDI stands for Universal Description, Discovery, and Integration. It is yet another XML grammar and accompanying API that is often included within the scope of Web Services technologies. UDDI is used to *publish* Web Services. That is, companies that maintain Web Services related to their business can publish information about the functionality and location of their services in a UDDI *registry* (a website that maintains a collection of UDDI documents about Web Services). Several major companies, including Microsoft (http://uddi.microsoft.com) and IBM (http://uddi.ibm.com), maintain large UDDI registries. Many companies and academic institutions will also have their own UDDI registries. You can search these registries via their Web interfaces in order to find existing Web Services that might suit your needs, as well as businesses that might be interested in using your services. In addition, you can publish information concerning services that you develop so that other people can locate and access them. Information made available via UDDI documents often includes the location of a WSDL contract for a Web Service in order to allow independent development of Web Service clients.

For more information on the UDDI grammar and on publishing J# Web Services using UDDI, please see ⌖JS060006.

Document versus RPC, Literal versus Encoded

SOAP messages can have one of two *encoding styles:*

- **Encoded** style follows the encoding rules specified in Section 7 of the SOAP specification (published by the W3C). Basically, the rules in Section 7 dictate the content of the SOAP <Body> element, and require that a data type be specified for each element included in a SOAP request or response message.
- **Literal** style does not follow the rules in any particular specification. The content of the <Body> element must be agreed upon and implemented in both the service and client implementations. Literal encoded SOAP messages do not necessarily specify a data type for each element, and it is usually up to the receiver to decide how each parameter should be translated into its own data types.

In addition, SOAP messages can follow one of two different *document styles:*

- In **RPC** style SOAP messages, the <Body> element contains a method name and parameters, and is understood to be a remote procedure call. In this case, the structure of the <Body> element follows rules laid out in Section 5 of the SOAP specification. If a Web Service is an RPC service, the client knows exactly how the data in its request messages will be handled by the service.
- In **Document** or **Message** style SOAP messages, the <Body> element is treated as an XML document. The structure of this

document must be agreed upon by client and service. In this case, the client does not know or care how the service will handle the information it receives; the client simply sends a message structured in the agreed-upon style and assumes that the service will know what to do with it.

By default, J# Web Services use the Literal encoding style, and Document-style messages. Most of the time this won't matter to you, as most languages that can interact with Web Services can handle Literal/Document encoding. In addition, the techniques we demonstrated in the "Making Web Services Cross-Language Compatible" section of this topic force your ASP.NET applications to generate RPC/Encoded style documents, in case you need to do so. RPC/Encoded style is another common combination of SOAP styles and is the default in many SOAP APIs, including Apache AXIS (a popular SOAP API for Java). Nevertheless, you may encounter communication problems when trying to integrate J# Web Services with other-language clients, or vice versa. For some tips and tricks on how to deal with these communication problems, please see ⌖JS060007.

SUMMARY

When designing a SOAP Web Service with the .NET Framework, most of the work is done for you under the hood. Starting a new ASP.NET Web Service generates a J# template that already has all the important Web-Service-specific code filled in. All you have to do is add functionality to the service, although it is sometimes necessary to add more tags in order to ensure that the Web Service is sending messages compatible with other SOAP implementations. ASP.NET Web Services are deployed automatically under the IIS Web Server when the project is built.

Remember that although ASP.NET Web Services use SOAP documents to send messages and WSDL contracts to describe themselves to potential clients, you never have to interact with SOAP or WSDL directly. Instead, you can think of writing a J# Web Service as writing a class library whose methods will be accessible over the World Wide Web.

Topic: Creating J# Web Service Clients

Creating a client in VS .NET in order to access a .NET Web Service is incredibly simple. Again, all the real work of sending HTTP/SOAP messages back and forth is done for you. All you have to do as the client developer is add a Web Reference to any service and then implement that service's methods in your code.

There are no templates for Web Service clients in VS .NET, but you will find that you do not need one. You can add a Web Reference to any project type in VS .NET, including Windows applications, console applications, class libraries, and even ASP.NET Web Applications or *other* ASP.NET Web Services. We will use only console and Windows desktop applications in this CodeNotes.

To start creating a Web Service client, you simply open Visual Studio .NET, start a new project (by clicking on the **New Project** button), and choose to create a new J# application (of any type). Don't forget to name the project before clicking **OK.** If you're not familiar with Windows applications and Windows Forms, we recommend that you read Chapter 4 of this CodeNotes before continuing with this topic.

CONCEPTS

Adding a Web Reference

To add a reference to an existing Web Service, select **Add Web Reference** from the Project menu in Visual Studio. This will open a new window named Add Web Reference. Type the URL of the Web Service you want to reference in the **Address** field and press the **Enter** key. If a Web Service exists at the URL you typed, VS .NET should locate the service and make available some information about it, as shown in Figure 6.8.

Note that you can also see a list of all Web Services on your local machine by clicking on the "Web services on the local machine" link when you first open the Add Web Reference window.

In the main panel of the Add Web Reference window in Figure 6.8, you can click on the links to view a WSDL contract (Service Description) of the Web Service. Note that the main panel is actually a Web browser containing the IIS Web Service interface you saw in the preceding topic, and that it also lists all the methods that are available in the Web Service you selected. You can click on a method name to see the format of SOAP and other messages that this service can send and receive.

You can also change the **Web Reference name** for your selected Web Service (localhost is the default and will work fine if you don't want to change it). This name will be used in your client code as a namespace representing the Web Service (you'll see what we mean subsequently).

Once you have located the service you want, click the **Add Reference** button to add a reference to the Web Service to your application. A

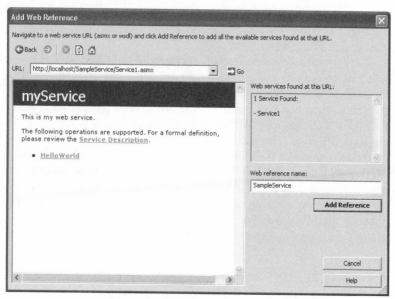

Figure 6.8 Adding a Web Reference

list of Web References will appear in the Solution Explorer (usually the top right panel in Visual Studio .NET) that includes the service you just added, as shown in Figure 6.9. Any methods available within this Web Service are now fully accessible within your application.

Invoking a Web Service

Create a new J# console application and add a reference to http://localhost/SampleService/Service1.asmx, as shown in Figure 6.8 in the previous section (if you're unsure of how to create a console application, please go back and read the "Simple Application" section in Chapter 3). You can then use the code shown in Listing 6.13 to invoke the Hello-World() method from that service and display its return message.

```
public static void main(String[] args)
{
 SampleService.myService ws = new SampleService.myService();
 System.out.println(ws.HelloWorld());
}
```

Listing 6.13 Invoking a Web Service

First we create a variable named ws that is an instance of the class that VS .NET has generated to represent SampleService. Then we can call

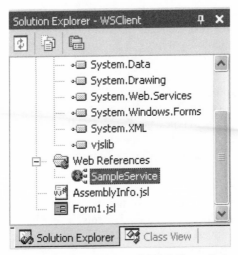

Figure 6.9 Solution Explorer with Web Reference listing

methods on ws and get return values from those methods, which can be used in our application. VS .NET encapsulates the Web Service as if it were a normal object. Therefore, we do not have to treat ws in a special way because it refers to a Web Service; we can treat it as we would any other object that has callable methods.

Exception Handling in Web Service Clients
When referencing a Web Service as shown in Listing 6.13 (also called using a wrapper or *proxy* class), you should account for the possibility that the underlying Web Service may not be available (that is, the connection may be down). It is therefore a good idea to use a try-catch block when making calls against the proxy class. If the service is not available for some reason, the .NET Framework will throw a WebException, so your try-catch block should look like Listing 6.14.

```
try
{
 SampleService.myService ws = new SampleService.myService();
 System.out.println(ws.HelloWorld());
}
catch (System.Net.WebException e)
{
 System.out.println("Web Service not available.");
}
```

Listing 6.14 Exception handling in a Web Service client

Note that we had to use the fully qualified name System.Net.WebException to catch a WebException in Listing 6.14. You can avoid using the fully qualified name by adding import System.Net.WebException; to the top of your class file.

Data Type Mappings

.NET Web Services (and clients) must be able to serialize and deserialize between .NET data types and SOAP (XML Schema) data types. This process is usually automated, and you do not need to provide any special type mappings in order for the conversions to take place.

Simple Data Types

Table 6.1 shows a list of some of the more commonly used .NET data types and their XML Schema equivalents. The .NET Framework will automatically convert between these data types when constructing and interpreting SOAP messages.

.NET Data Type	XML Schema Data Type
System.Uri	anyURI
System.Boolean	Boolean
System.DateTime	dateTime, date, gDay, gYear, etc. (see below)
System.Decimal	decimal, integer
System.Double	Double
System.String	String (see below)
System.Int32	Int
System.Int64	Long

Table 6.1 NET/SOAP type mappings

Note that some Framework data types can be converted into more than one XML Schema data type, depending on the circumstances. For example, if a DateTime contained only year information, it might be converted to an XML Schema gYear.

You can find a complete list of .NET Framework–to–XML Schema data type mappings at ⌐⟳JS060008.

Complex Data Types

Encoding complex data types in .NET is slightly more involved and often differs depending on whether you are using default .NET Document/Literal encoding or SOAP RPC encoding (see the "Document versus RPC, Literal versus Encoded" design note in the previous topic). Arrays of strings, doubles, integers, and other simple data types will be converted automatically into array structures in SOAP messages, regardless of the encoding being used. ArrayList objects will also be converted automatically into SOAP arrays. You can use arrays and ArrayLists as you normally would in your .NET applications and assume that they will be serialized correctly.

.NET also knows how to serialize Framework classes into special sets of SOAP elements called *structs*. A struct is like an array, except that each element in it is identified by a name instead of a number. The best way to have a data type serialize to a struct in J# is simply to create a new class whose variables will represent the keys in the struct. When serialization occurs, .NET generates a struct in the SOAP document with the variable names as accessors and the variable values as values. The following example (see Web link) will demonstrate this technique.

EXAMPLE

Due to space constraints in this book, we have placed the example for this topic online. Please see ⊶JS060009 for an example of a J# Windows desktop client for the Web Service we produced in the example from the previous topic (⊶JS060005).

HOW AND WHY

How Do I Write a Client for Someone Else's Web Service?

In this chapter, we showed you how to write your own Web Services and then how to write your own clients to access them. This is often sufficient, especially if you want to be the only distributor of client applications for your particular service. However, many Web Service programmers publish their Web Services on the Web and then expect people interested in using the Web Service to write their own clients. Alternatively, some Web Services have very specific functionality (e.g., there might be a Web Service that returns the temperature at a given global location), and you may simply want to integrate such a service into a larger, existing application.

You can write J# clients for any existing Web Service, no matter what language it is written in, with only one stipulation: the Web Service *must* have a publicly available WSDL contract. There are several locations on the Web where you can find lists of available services and their WSDL contracts. Two of these are the UDDI registries discussed earlier in this chapter, and XMethods (www.xmethods.com), a website that maintains a large list of public Web Services for which anyone can write clients. For a complete example of how to write a J# client for someone else's Web Service, please see ⟜JS060010.

How Do I Change the Name of My Web Service after I've Built It?

As you may recall, you must select the location of your Web Service when you first start the project. The name of the service itself always starts as Service1.asmx. In order to change this you need to rename the class and its constructor method in the code for the service, and then re-name the .asmx file itself, which can be done from the Solution Explorer in VS .NET or from Windows Explorer.

In order to move the service to a different address (that is, to change it from http://localhost/MyService/Service1.asmx to http://localhost/SomeOtherService/Service1.asmx), you will need to create a new virtual directory in IIS and then copy the required files into the new directory manually. ⟜JS060011 has a detailed example of moving and renaming a Web Service project.

SUMMARY

A Web Service client in .NET must add a Web Reference to an existing Web Service (you add a Web Reference by selecting **Project → Add Web Reference** in Visual Studio .NET). When you add a Web Reference, Visual Studio .NET creates a local class that represents the Web Service class. This class can be treated exactly as though it were a normal, local class; all networking and cross-Web communication code is generated automatically behind the scenes.

Once you have a Web Reference, the client will be able to access the methods and data types made available though the Web Service's WSDL contract. Remember that J# Web Service clients can be written for a Web Service only if that service has a WSDL contract available. Beyond the initial Web Reference, writing a client application (which can use any of the .NET templates) requires no special code. All conversion of data types to and from SOAP is done automatically by the ASP.NET engine.

Chapter Summary

Writing a Web Service in .NET is extremely easy because .NET does most of the work behind the scenes. Web Services are written by using

Visual Studio .NET and by using Simple Object Access Protocol (SOAP) to send and receive messages. Classes and methods are made available over the Web by attaching special ASP.NET attribute tags such as /** @attribute WebService() */ or /** @attribute WebService() */. These attributes allow you to provide namespace and encoding information and to indicate that classes and methods should be made public on the Web.

.NET Web Service clients need only provide a Web Reference to an existing service in order to invoke its methods. Adding a Web Reference causes Visual Studio .NET to create a local class representing the Web Service class. The local class contains all the necessary information to construct and interpret Web Service messages. It is also responsible for forwarding the information between the client and the server, thus eliminating the need for the client to construct calls and interact directly with the service. .NET Web Services automatically generate WSDL documents to which Web References can be added. It is not possible to write a J# client for a Web Service that does not publish a WSDL contract.

Microsoft has an extensive database of articles and information on creating and maintaining Web Services in .NET. You will find a list of links to relevant topics on Microsoft's Web Services pages at CodeNotes Pointer ⌖JS060013.

Chapter 7

—

J# MARINE BIOLOGY SIMULATION
CASE STUDY

The Marine Biology Simulation (MBS) Case Study is an opportunity for students in Advanced Placement Computer Science classes to gain experience developing J# in a larger-scale application. Although the case study is geared toward advanced high school students, it offers many interesting opportunities for anyone learning the Java language or just object-oriented programming in general. The case study follows the experiences of a computer science student named Pat during a summer job at a marine biology firm. The application Pat is working on, which is the focus of the MBS Case Study, is a simulator that allows marine biologists to model the behavior of various kinds of fish in a bounded or unbounded grid (intended to represent an aquatic environment).

The original MBS and its accompanying case study were developed in C++ and then in Java by programmers at the College Board, a nonprofit educational organization. Microsoft, in preparation for the 2003–2004 school year, has developed a J# version of the MBS that functions in an identical manner but takes advantage of the graphical capabilities of Windows Forms rather than the Java Swing GUI library. In order to follow along with this chapter, you will need to have the J# version of the Marine Biology Case Study installed, as detailed in Chapter 2 of this CodeNotes. We also recommend that you read the case study documentation before continuing with this chapter, in order to familiarize yourself with the MBS application. This chapter is not meant to be complete documentation of the case study, but rather a supplementary introduction to working with it in J# and Visual Studio .NET.

Chapter 7 is divided into three sections. The "Simple Application" and "Core Concepts" sections will introduce you to the J# MBS and provide an example of how to use the simulator in its default form (that is, without making any changes to the original J# solution). In the first topic, "Customizing the Case Study in Visual Studio .NET," we will modify the application by adding a new breed of fish to the simulator, in order to demonstrate techniques for working with larger solutions in Visual Studio .NET. In the second topic, "Extending the Case Study," we will take advantage of some additional Visual Studio .NET features and create a Web Service that will allow clients to get some statistics on a simulation over the Web.

Again, keep in mind that you should be somewhat familiar with the original case study documentation before reading this chapter. In particular, you should have read Chapter 4 of the documentation, which details the addition of specialized fish to the simulator. You can find links to the documentation and case study versions at ⟨CN⟩JS070001.

Simple Application

In this simple application, we will explore Microsoft's J# implementation of the Marine Biology Simulation. Remember that you need to have installed the MBS as detailed in Chapter 2.

The MBS Case Study Solution

Open Visual Studio .NET and select the **Open Project** button. Browse to the directory in which you installed the code for the MBS Case Study. If you installed to the default directory, the MBS will be located in C:\Program Files\MBS Case Study for Visual J# .NET\Code. Select the file Marine Biology Simulation.sln and click **Open** to open the project in Visual Studio .NET.

All the files for the MBS will be available in the Solution Explorer. One thing you may notice is that there are many more files available in the J# version than there were in the Java language version. This is because in the Java language version, many of the files that were not intended to be edited were "black boxed" inside a JAR (Java Archive) file. Microsoft has elected to leave all files in the J# version in unarchived form rather than compile them into assemblies. However, in order to remain inside the bounds of the case study documentation, you should only edit the files found in the MBSCore folder, shown in Figure 7.1, and the MBSGUI folder.

Starting the GUI

The J# MBS comes ready to run. Press **CTRL + F5** to compile and run the Marine Biology Simulator. Because of its size, the MBS will take longer to compile than the other applications with which you have worked in this CodeNotes. You will eventually be presented with the window in Figure 7.2. This is the initial MBS screen.

The interface for the MBS in J# is almost identical to that of the original version, except for a few extra options under the View menu. These extra options are aesthetic in nature and allow you to change the background colors of the simulator and its contents, as well as view the grid in full-screen mode.

The Environment

Open the **File** menu and select **Create New Environment.** You will be presented with the window in Figure 7.3.

Figure 7.1 Core files in J# MBS Case Study

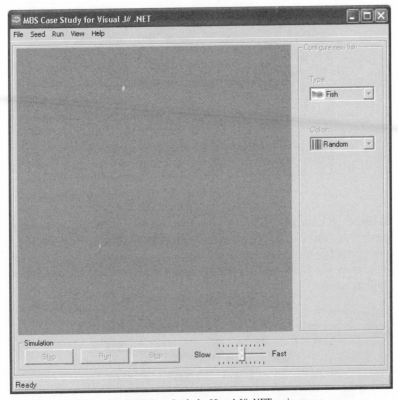

Figure 7.2 MBS Case Study for Visual J# .NET main screen

From the Create New Environment window, you can choose to create two different kinds of environments for your fish to swim in. In a *bounded environment,* the fish have a set number of grid squares in which to move around. You can assign a number of rows and columns to the environment using the Rows and Columns fields, and the fish will not be able to leave these boundaries. You can also create an *unbounded environment,* in which fish can swim wherever they please and the environment is virtually limitless (only to the extent of your system's memory, of course). For this simple application, we will use a bounded environment. Leave the Rows and Columns fields at 10 (their default values), and click the **Create** button to create a 10×10, 100-square grid, as shown in Figure 7.4.

Adding Fish
Now it is time to add some fish to our environment. Click on the arrow next to the Type drop-down menu in order to see a list of available fish,

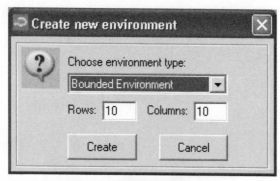

Figure 7.3 The Create New Environment window

as shown in Figure 7.5. One thing you may notice is that there are a few more fish available in the J# MBS than there were in the original version. In addition to the ordinary Fish, you can select a DarterFish (which moves more quickly but only in a straight line) or a SlowFish (which has only a one in five chance of moving). Both DarterFish and

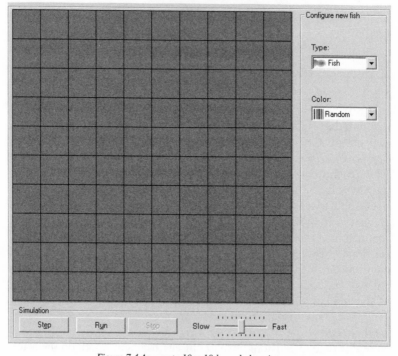

Figure 7.4 An empty 10 × 10 bounded environment

SlowFish are discussed in Chapter 4 of the original MBS Case Study documentation. Microsoft has also included two more fish in its J# MBS: BnDFish is a fish that can breed and die, as discussed in Chapter 3 of the MBS Case Study documentation. ImageFish is a fish for which you can customize the GIF used to represent it on the grid. You can find a further discussion of BnDFish and ImageFish at ᴄᴺ JS070002.

In order to add a fish, click on a fish type in the Type drop-down menu, and then click on any grid square. An image representing the fish type you selected will appear in the square on which you clicked. Click on the fish again to turn it 90 degrees clockwise—this allows you to set the initial direction of the fish. To remove a fish from the grid, keep clicking on it until it turns all the way around, and then it will disappear. Add 10 fish of different types to your grid so it looks something like Figure 7.6.

You can hover your mouse arrow over any fish in the grid to see some information about it, including its fish type, its location on the grid, the direction in which it is facing, and its unique ID number (used by the application to identify individual fish). For example, Figure 7.7 shows what you would see if you hovered your mouse over the SlowFish in the bottom row of the grid in Figure 7.6.

Running the Simulation

Our simulation is ready to run. Click the **Run** button at the bottom of the MBS window to start the simulation. The fish in the grid will start to move, and you will be able to see how each different type of fish acts (SlowFish will rarely move, DarterFish will dart back and forth, etc.). If you put BnDFish in your environment (as we did in Figure 7.6), you may see them die (disappear) or breed multiple new fish.

You can change the speed of the simulation by moving the slider at the bottom of the MBS window between **Slow** and **Fast.** Remember that

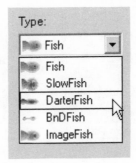

Figure 7.5 The Fish type drop-down

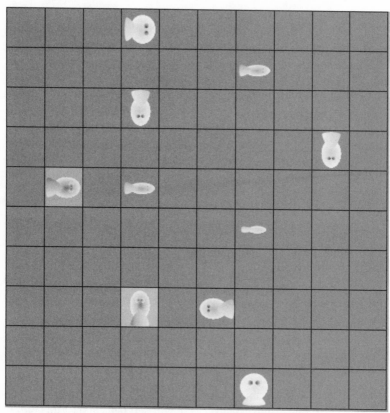

Figure 7.6 Some fish in a 10 × 10 grid

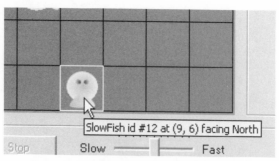

Figure 7.7 Getting information about a fish in the grid

the faster you ask the simulation to run, the more taxing it will be on your machine—if you have a lot of fish and a slow machine, you might find that increasing the speed of the simulation has very little effect or bogs down your machine's processor.

Stop the simulation at any time by clicking the **Stop** button. When the simulation is stopped, you will again be able to hold your mouse cursor over fish in the grid to see information about them. You can also use the **Step** button to have every fish in the grid go through one movement cycle (remember that not all fish will move every movement cycle— SlowFish will move only once every five clicks of the **Step** button, on average). While the simulation is stopped, you can add more fish to the grid.

Although there are other aspects of the MBS with which you can experiment, our current demonstration is complete. To ensure that you can come back later to the simulation you just created, open the File menu and select **Save.** You will be asked to give your environment a name and to select a location in which to save it. MBS environment files have the file extension .dat and by default are located in the MBS Case Study for Visual J# .NET\DataFiles directory. Select **Quit** from the File menu to exit the MBS.

CORE CONCEPTS

Advanced Placement Computer Science Course
The Marine Biology Simulation Case Study is the major case study used in the Advanced Placement (AP) Computer Science course. The AP program offers a large selection of college-level courses to advanced students in many American high schools. It is sponsored by a nonprofit organization called the College Board, whose home page is located at www.collegeboard.com.

According to the AP Computer Science 2003 Course Description, the AP Computer Science course is divided into two sections: Computer Science A "emphasizes programming methodology with a concentration on problem solving and algorithm development and is meant to be the equivalent of a first-semester course in Computer Science." Computer Science AB "includes all of the topics of Computer Science A, as well as a more formal and in-depth study of algorithms, data structures, and abstraction." AP students and teachers for both the A and the AB courses who are reading this CodeNotes will already be familiar with many aspects of the original Java or C++ versions of the MBS Case Study. As mentioned previously, this chapter is meant to supplement that case study by showing how Microsoft has implemented it in .NET and how the simulation can be expanded upon by using the Visual Studio .NET development environment and technologies in the BCL.

If you are reading this CodeNotes and you are *not* an AP Computer Science student or teacher, you will still find this chapter extremely useful. You can find links to descriptions of the AP Computer Science curriculum and to downloadable versions of the J# MBS Case Study and code at ⌕JS070001. We highly recommend that you read through this case study before continuing with this chapter. For example, we will assume you already know about the important classes in the case study (environment classes, fish classes, etc.). Even if you are not an AP Computer Science student, you will find that the J# Marine Biology Case Study is a good tool for learning about large-scale J# and .NET development in the real world.

Topic: Customizing the Case Study in Visual Studio .NET

Visual Studio .NET makes modifying and customizing your J# projects very easy. The documentation for the original version of the Marine Biology Simulation Case Study details how to add two new kinds of fish to the simulation (DarterFish and SlowFish). In this topic, we will use the Visual Studio .NET IDE to add another new type of fish and show how to integrate that fish into the MBS Windows GUI. Our new fish is called HungryFish. A HungryFish lies in wait on the grid for an unsuspecting fish to pass by; when another type of fish moves next to HungryFish, HungryFish will eat it and move into the victim's square on the grid. Read on to find out how to add predators to your J# Marine Biology Simulation.

CORE CONCEPTS

Creating the HungryFish Class
The first thing we need to do is add a new class file to our application. As mentioned at the beginning of this chapter, most of the files you will need to edit are located in the MBSCore folder in the Solution Explorer. Expand this folder by clicking the "+" icon next to it, and you will see a list of classes that includes all the fish classes (Fish, DarterFish, SlowFish, etc.) as well as some additional environment and simulation classes that are discussed in the case study documentation.

Right-click on MBSCore in the Solution Explorer and select **Add** → **Add New Item**. Select the J# Class template, and name it Hungry-Fish.java. Note that we are giving our new class the .java extension so that it fits in with the rest of the classes in the MBSCore folder (the classes in MBSCore were imported from the original Java language MBS). We could call our new class HungryFish.jsl and it would work just as well. Click the **Open** button to add HungryFish.java to the MBSCore folder.

Open HungryFish in the Visual Studio .NET code editor by double-clicking on it in the Solution Explorer. You will notice that Visual Studio .NET has included some default code that declares the HungryFish class, gives it a default constructor, and puts it in a package called MBSCore. For the purposes of this example it is easier to start from scratch, so erase all of the code and make HungryFish.java completely blank.

Import Statements
Add the import statements in Listing 7.1 to the top of HungryFish.java.

```
import java.awt.Color;
import java.util.ArrayList;
import java.util.Random;
```

Listing 7.1 Import statements for HungryFish

We will need these three utility classes in order to make HungryFish work. Specifically, Color will be used to specify the color of the image used to represent a HungryFish, ArrayList will be used to represent a HungryFish's neighboring grid cells, and Random will be used to provide a random likelihood of a HungryFish's eating another fish. We will explain all of these classes in more detail as we come across them.

The HungryFish Class
Our HungryFish class needs to inherit from the default Fish class. This will allow us to override only methods that apply to HungryFish's special behavior (eating other fish), and to use the default movement and direction functions from the original Fish class without having to rewrite them. Add the code in Listing 7.2 to HungryFish.java, after the import statements.

```
public class HungryFish extends Fish
{
}
```

Listing 7.2 The HungryFish class

The probOfEating Method

When a `HungryFish` has neighbors on the grid, there is a certain probability that it will eat one of those neighbors and move into the neighbor's space on the grid. This probability is represented by `probOfEating`, a private global variable. Add the line in Listing 7.3 inside the `HungryFish` class.

```
private double probOfEating;
```

Listing 7.3 probOfEating

We will assign a value to `probOfEating` in the `HungryFish` constructors.

HungryFish Constructors

All fish classes have three constructors. All three constructors require an `Environment` and a `Location` object as first and second parameters, respectively. These parameters allow the fish to be created in a specified environment (that is, the one that is currently visible in the simulator), and in a specified location on the grid (that is, the cell on which you clicked to add the fish). However, the constructors differ in the following ways:

- The first constructor requires only the `Environment` and `Location` objects. It generates a random direction and color for the fish.
- The second constructor requires an `Environment` object, a `Location` object, and a `Direction` object specifying a direction (e.g., NORTH, SOUTH, EAST, or WEST). The fish's color is still generated randomly.
- The third constructor requires a `Color` object in addition to the other three parameters, which allows the object creator to specify a color for the fish.

We need to override all three of these constructors from the parent `Fish` class. Each constructor needs to call the equivalent parent constructor, which will add a new fish to the environment. However, each constructor also needs to assign a value to `probOfEating`. This value will be used to determine the likelihood that a `HungryFish` will eat its neighbor. We want `HungryFish` to have a one in three chance of eating, so the three `HungryFish` constructors should look like Listing 7.4.

```
public HungryFish(Environment env, Location loc)
{
  super(env, loc, env.randomDirection(), Color.red);
  probOfEating = 1.0/3.0;
```

```
}

public HungryFish(Environment env, Location loc, Direction
    dir)
 {
  super(env, loc, dir, Color.red);
  probOfEating = 1.0/3.0;
 }

public HungryFish(Environment env, Location loc,
  Direction dir, Color col)
{
 super(env, loc, dir, col);
 probOfEating = 1.0/3.0;
}
```

Listing 7.4 HungryFish constructors

Our HungryFish class is set up, and we are ready to add the eating functionality.

Making HungryFish Eat
At this point, HungryFish is almost identical to an ordinary Fish. It is now time to override some important methods from the parent Fish class in order to give HungryFish the ability to eat.

The move() Method
The first method we need to override is the move() method, which is responsible for actually moving the fish from its current location to a new one. The default move() method is relatively simple. It starts out by calling the nextLocation() method in order to determine where (if anywhere) the fish will move next. We will look at nextLocation() (which also must be overridden) in the next section. For now, understand that nextLocation() may return a new location into which the fish can move, or it may simply return the current location of the fish. If nextLocation() returns a new location, the move() method moves the fish to that new location (by calling a method named changeLocation() that is inherited from Fish). If nextLocation() returns the fish's current location, move() generates a random direction and points the fish in that direction. Therefore, a HungryFish that does not find prey in one direction might turn around to look for food in another direction.

The new move() method, which you should add to the HungryFish class, is shown in Listing 7.5.

```
protected void move()
{
  // Find a location to move to.
  Debug.print("HungryFish " + toString() +
        " attempting to move. ");
  Location nextLoc = nextLocation();

  // If the next location is different, move there.
  if ( ! nextLoc.equals(location()) )
  {
    changeLocation(nextLoc);
    Debug.println(" Moves to " + location());
  }
  else
  {
    // Otherwise, reverse direction.
    Direction d = direction().randomDirection();
    d = d.roundedDir(4, direction().NORTH);
    changeDirection(d);
    Debug.println(" Now facing " + direction());
  }
}
```

Listing 7.5 The move() method

Note that each time a fish attempts to move, actually does move, or changes direction, we also output a message to the debugger in order to make it easier to trace what is going on behind the scenes. You can find out how to view these messages while the MBS application is running at ☜JS070003.

The nextLocation() Method

The nextLocation() method is responsible for determining the next grid cell into which a fish will move (if it moves at all). As mentioned previously, nextLocation() can return either a new location or the current location of a fish.

The nextLocation() method starts by obtaining an ArrayList representing all the occupied neighbors of the HungryFish (that is, all neighboring cells containing edible fish). This ArrayList is obtained by using the fullNeighbors() method (which we will discuss in the next section), and may have anywhere from 0 to 8 members, depending on how crowded the HungryFish's area is. The nextLocation() method then removes the location directly behind the fish from the ArrayList, as a

HungryFish cannot move backward or eat fish that are directly behind it. Finally, nextLocation() calls the eats() method in order to determine whether the HungryFish will eat a neighbor (we will look at the eats() method subsequently). If the HungryFish does eat, nextLocation() picks a random neighbor fish, removes that neighbor from the grid, and then returns the neighbor's location to the calling method (move()). In other words, when HungryFish eats, it moves into the square where its prey used to be. When HungryFish does not eat, nextLocation() simply returns its current location.

Add the code for nextLocation(), shown in Listing 7.6, to Hungry-Fish.java.

```
protected Location nextLocation()
{
// find full neighbors
ArrayList fullNbrs = fullNeighbors();

// remove location behind
Direction oppositeDir = direction().reverse();
Location locationBehind =
      environment().getNeighbor(location(), oppositeDir);
if (fullNbrs.contains(locationBehind))
 fullNbrs.remove(fullNbrs.indexOf(locationBehind));

if (eats(fullNbrs))
 {
 Random randNumGen = RandNumGenerator.get Instance();
 int randNum = randNumGen.nextInt(fullNbrs.size());
 Location eatLoc = (Location)fullNbrs.get(randNum);
 environment().remove(environment().objectAt(eatLoc));
 return eatLoc;
 }

 return location();
}
```

Listing 7.6 nextLocation()

For more information on how to use the random number generator in J#, please see ⊶ᴺᴶS070004.

The fullNeighbors() Method

The fullNeighbors() method is a helper method that returns an Array-List of all the occupied neighbor cells of the cell that a HungryFish currently occupies. This ArrayList is used as a list of possible targets for the HungryFish to eat. Add the code for fullNeighbors(), shown in Listing 7.7, to HungryFish.java.

```
protected ArrayList fullNeighbors()
{
  // Get all the neighbors of this fish, full or not.
  ArrayList nbrs = environment().neighborsOf(location());
  // Figure out which neighbors are full and add to a list
  ArrayList fullNbrs = new ArrayList();
  for ( int index = 0; index < nbrs.size(); index++ )
  {
   Location loc = (Location) nbrs.get(index);
   if ( !environment().isEmpty(loc) )
    fullNbrs.add(loc);
  }

  return fullNbrs;
}
```

Listing 7.7 The fullNeighbors() *method*

The eats() Method

Finally, we need to create the eats() method, which is unique to HungryFish, as none of the other currently implemented fish eats its neighbors. The eats() method is responsible for determining whether a HungryFish will eat (and therefore move). The eats() method returns true when the HungryFish eats, and false when it does not.

The first thing eats() does is to determine whether any of the HungryFish's occupied neighbors are fellow HungryFish. Because we don't want our HungryFish to be a cannibal, the eats() method removes any neighboring HungryFish from the list of possible targets before determining whether or not it eats. If there are no remaining occupied neighbors, the eats() method immediately returns false. If there are still potential targets in neighboring cells, the eats() method uses the probOfEating variable we defined earlier in order to determine randomly whether the HungryFish will eat. There is a one in three chance that eats() will return true if there are any occupied, non-HungryFish neighbors.

Add the code in Listing 7.8 to the HungryFish class.

```
protected boolean eats(ArrayList fullNbrs)
{
  for (int i = fullNbrs.size()-1;i>=0;i--)
  {
```

```
Location loc = (Location)fullNbrs.get(i);
String nbrType =
    environment().objectAt(loc).getClass().getName();
if (nbrType.equals("HungryFish"))
fullNbrs.remove(fullNbrs.indexOf(loc));
}
if (fullNbrs.size() == 0)
return false;

Random randNumGen = RandNumGenerator.getInstance();
if ( randNumGen.nextDouble() < probOfKilling )
return true;

return false;
}
```

Listing 7.8 The eats() *method*

Our HungryFish class is complete. The final task is to make HungryFish available in the MBS GUI.

Adding HungryFish to the MBS GUI

We need to make HungryFish available in the list of fish types in the MBS GUI. Expand the MBS GUI folder in the Solution Explorer and locate the file GUIForm.jsl. This is a new file in the J# version of the MBS application, which represents the main GUI window that we saw back in Figure 7.2 at the beginning of this chapter. Double-click on GUIForm.jsl. By default, it will open in the design view and you will be able to look at the form itself. Double-click anywhere on the form to open its Code-Behind, and scroll down to the bottom of the code to locate the main() method. It is in the main() method that we add HungryFish to the GUI.

You will need to make five changes to the main() method:

1. Underneath the five lines beginning with DisplayMap.associate, add the line of code in Listing 7.9.

```
DisplayMap.associate("HungryFish", new NarrowFishDisplay());
```

Listing 7.9 Linking HungryFish *to the display*

This line of code associates HungryFish with a particular display method (NarrowFishDisplay()), which is responsible for determining how it appears on the grid. Note that in order to maintain simplicity in this example, our HungryFish will use the same display method as DarterFish.

2. Change the line `String[] FishNameArray = new String[5];` to read `String[] FishNameArray = new String[6];`. This array will be used to populate the `Type` list box in the GUI.

3. Add the line in Listing 7.10 after the five existing `FishNameArray` declarations.

```
FishNameArray[5] = "HungryFish";
```

Listing 7.10 Adding the `FishName`

4. Change the line `Image[] FishImageArray = new Image[5];` to read `Image[] FishImageArray = new Image[6];`. This array holds references to the images used to represent each fish.

5. Add the line in Listing 7.11 after the five existing `FishImageArray` declarations.

```
FishImageArray[5] = (Image)resMan.GetObject("darter.gif");
```

Listing 7.11 Adding an image for the fish

For more information on the `Image` class in J#, please see ⟨CN⟩JS070005.

`HungryFish` will now be available in the MBS GUI. Run the application by pressing **CTRL + F5,** create a new bounded environment, and add some fish to it just as you did in the simple application. This time, however, include some `HungryFish` in your simulation. Click the **Start** button to watch them devour the other fish!

DESIGN NOTES

A More Realistic Simulation

Although our `HungryFish` will eat its neighbors, a more realistic simulation would require that we cause `HungryFish` to die if it *doesn't eat* within a fixed number of moves. After all, a predator fish that eats all of its neighbors won't survive very long. With the addition of a static variable, a few code checks in the `eat()` method, and some functionality from the `BnDFish`, we can create a much more realistic predator fish. See ⟨CN⟩JS070009 for some starter code.

SUMMARY

Adding a fish to the Marine Biology Case Study is an interesting exercise in object-oriented programming. Not only are you inheriting behavior from a base class (Fish), you are also modifying and extending the behavior by overriding methods and adding new functions. As long as your modified fish inherits from Fish and follows the rules for implementing the required methods, you can create any new functionality you wish. In the next topic, we will look beyond the basic case study and see how we can add entirely new features to the basic functions.

Topic: Extending the Case Study

Because the J# Marine Biology Case Study is a solution in Visual Studio .NET, it is possible to add code to it that will allow you to take advantage of the wide variety of classes in the Base Class Library. Some examples of extensions to the MBS Case Study could include writing code to allow environment files to be stored in a database rather than as simple text files or creating a Web GUI for the MBS by leveraging ASP.NET. Because J# is a fully supported .NET language, all of the classes in the .NET Framework are available to it.

In this chapter, we will extend the MBS Case Study by creating a Web Service that will allow MBS users to share environment information over the Web. The Web Service will have two Web Methods:

- getFileList() Returns an array of strings representing all the environment data files available on the Web Service host's machine.
- getEnv() Returns environment data from a specified .dat file. This environment data will be stored in a custom class called SerializableEnvironment, which we will also show you how to create in this topic. Environment data returned by getEnv() can be deserialized by the client and used to construct an environment on the Web Service client's machine.

Our Web Service client, in this example, will be the MBS application itself. We will add a new menu option, Import Environment from the Web, to the File menu in the MBS GUI. This option will allow users to select from a list of environments on a remote machine (this list is obtained using getFileList()). When the user selects an environment, the client will download the environment data from the Web Service using getEnv() and use the environment data to populate a new environment in the GUI.

You can find complete code for the Web Service, as well as the code that will be added to the MBS Case Study solution, at ⚓JS070006. If you are not familiar with Web Services and have not yet read Chapter 6 of this CodeNotes, we recommend that you go back and do so before continuing with this chapter.

CORE CONCEPTS

Creating the Web Service

We will create our Web Service in a solution separate from the MBS GUI. Open Visual Studio .NET and select **New Project.** Choose the J# Web Service template, and call your Web Service MBSEnvironmentService. Be sure to leave the http://localhost/ section of the address as is. Click **OK,** and Visual Studio .NET will generate a new Web Service solution, including a default .asmx page (Service1.asmx).

Click on the "click here to switch to code view" link to open the CodeBehind for Service1.asmx. As usual, Visual Studio .NET has generated some default code. Most of the code is necessary (although we'll make some changes to it in a moment), but you can erase the default "HelloWorld" Web method and the comments that surround it.

Before we start writing Web Methods, we are going to rename our .asmx file and Web Service class to something more descriptive than Service1. Right-click on Service1.asmx in the Solution Explorer and select **Rename.** Rename the file Environments.asmx. In the code for Environments.asmx (which should already be open), change the name of the main public class to Environments. You will also need to change the name of the class's constructor to Environments() instead of Service1(). You will now be able to type the URL http://localhost/MBSEnvironmentService/Environments.asmx into a Web browser to access your Web Service class and its methods.

Finally, add a WebService attribute before the Environments class declaration that places your Web Service in the http://www.codenotes.com namespace. Your code window should then look something like Figure 7.8.

We're now ready to start adding Web Methods to our Web Service class.

The getFileList() Method

Our first Web Service method, getFileList(), will return an array of strings representing all the .dat files available on the Web Service's host machine. The getFileList() method is extremely simple, but before we can write it we need to add the additional import statement in Listing 7.12 to the top of the code.

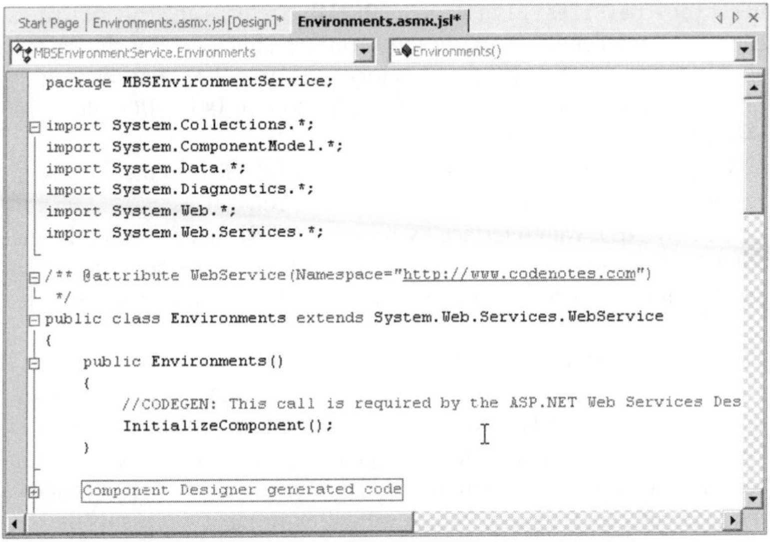

```
Start Page | Environments.asmx.jsl [Design]* | Environments.asmx.jsl* |          ◁ ▷ ×

MBSEnvironmentService.Environments        ▼    ⚬ Environments()                  ▼

      package MBSEnvironmentService;

    import System.Collections.*;
    import System.ComponentModel.*;
    import System.Data.*;
    import System.Diagnostics.*;
    import System.Web.*;
    import System.Web.Services.*;

    /** @attribute WebService(Namespace="http://www.codenotes.com")
     */
    public class Environments extends System.Web.Services.WebService
    {
        public Environments()
        {
            //CODEGEN: This call is required by the ASP.NET Web Services Des
            InitializeComponent();            I
        }

        Component Designer generated code
```

Figure 7.8 The CodeBehind for Environments.asmx (before Web Methods are added)

```
import System.IO.*;
```

Listing 7.12 Importing the System.IO namespace

The System.IO namespace contains classes for dealing with files, directory structures, and streams of data. Because getFileList() needs access to a directory in order to find all the .dat files, System.IO is necessary.

We can now write the getFileList() method, which contains only two lines of code. Add the method in Listing 7.13 to the Environments class.

```
/** @attribute WebMethod()
 */
public String[] getFileList()
{
 String[] dataList = Directory.GetFiles
("C:\\Program Files\\MBS Case Study" +
  "for Visual J# .NET\\DataFiles");
 return dataList;
}
```

Listing 7.13 The getFileList() method

`Directory.GetFiles()` is a static method that returns an array of strings, each one representing a file in the specified directory. For the sake of simplicity, we hard-coded the directory in Listing 7.13. For an example of a better way to locate and specify a directory in J# file I/O, please see ⟨CN⟩JS070007.

In Listing 7.13, we made `getFileList()` available over the Web by appending a `WebMethod` attribute to the top of it. You can test `getFileList()` in the ASP.NET Web interface by pressing **CTRL + F5.** Select the **get-FileList** link, and then click the **Invoke** button on the next page. Your service should return an XML file similar to the one in Figure 7.9.

The getEnv() Method

Now that our clients can use `getFileList()` to find out what data files are available, we need to create a Web Method that will allow them to access the contents of these files. The `getEnv()` method takes a string representing a file name as a parameter and returns a custom object called a `SerializableEnvironment` (which we will write) that represents the data from the selected environment data file. Before writing the code for `getEnv()`, we first need to construct the `SerializableEnvironment` class.

SerializableEnvironment

Add the code in Listing 7.14 to the very end of `Environments.asmx`, *after* the final bracket of the `Environments` class.

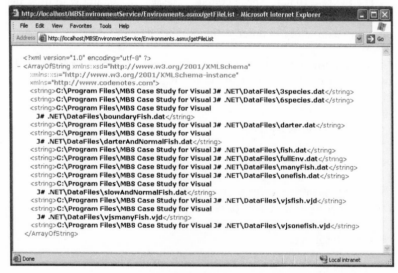

Figure 7.9 The output from `getFileList()` *in the ASP.NET Web interface*

```
class SerializableEnvironment
{
 public String envType;
 public int rows;
 public int cols;
 public Object[] myFishList;
}
```

Listing 7.14 The `SerializableEnvironment` *class*

The `SerializableEnvironment` class has four public variables: a `String` that represents the environment type ("bounded" or "unbounded"), two integers that represent the number of rows and columns in the environment grid (if it is a bounded environment), and an array of `Objects` that represent the fish in the list. We will create an instance of `SerializableEnvironment` in the `getEnv()` method and return it to the client that called the Web Service.

Back to getEnv()

Now that the `SerializableEnvironment` custom class is available, we can go back and write a `getEnv()` method that returns environment information to the client.

Start by declaring the `getEnv()` method, shown in Listing 7.15, inside the `Environments` class.

```
/** @attribute WebMethod()
 */
public SerializableEnvironment getEnv(String envFileString)
{
}
```

Listing 7.15 The `getEnv( )` *method declaration*

As previously mentioned, `getEnv()` is a public Web Method that accepts a `String` representing a data file name and returns a `SerializableEnvironment` containing the data found in the provided file. Inside `getEnv()`, add the three lines of code in Listing 7.16.

```
SerializableEnvironment sEnv = new SerializableEnvironment();
FileInfo envFile = new FileInfo(envFileString);
StreamReader reader = new StreamReader(envFile.OpenRead());
```

Listing 7.16 First three lines of `getEnv( )`

The sEnv variable, a SerializableEnvironment, will be populated with data from the environment data file and used as a return value. Our env-File variable is an instance of FileInfo representing the data file we will be working with. The reader variable is a StreamReader that will allow us to read through envFile one line at a time, in order to parse the data file's data into the appropriate structures.

Parsing the File

The first line of any environment data file specifies environment type (bounded or unbounded) and the width and height of the environment if applicable. For example, the first line in 3species.dat (a bounded environment file) looks like Listing 7.17.

```
bounded 12 12
```

Listing 7.17 The first line of a sample .dat file

In order to extract the first line of an environment data file into .NET Framework data types and add it to the SerializableEnvironment(sEnv), add the code in Listing 7.18 to the getEnv() method.

```
String envDef = reader.ReadLine();
String splitter = " ";
String[] envDefArray = envDef.Split(splitter.toCharArray());

sEnv.envType = envDefArray[0];
if (sEnv.envType.equals("bounded"))
{
 sEnv.rows = Integer.parseInt(envDefArray[1]);
 sEnv.cols = Integer.parseInt(envDefArray[2]);
}
else
{
 sEnv.rows = -1;
 sEnv.cols = -1;
}
```

Listing 7.18 Extracting the environment type and size from the data file

The code in Listing 7.18 uses the StreamReader to read the first line of the .dat file into a String. We then parse the parts of the string into an array. This array (envDefArray) will have either one or three elements, depending upon whether the environment file represents a bounded or unbounded environment. We then store the extracted values in the appropriate public variables in sEnv. Note that in Listing 7.18 we use a special method named

`Integer.parseInt()` to convert the strings extracted from the `.dat` file into `int` data types. If we're dealing with an unbounded environment, there will be no row or column values in the data file, so we assign `-1` (an obviously invalid value) to `sEnv.rows` and `sEnv.cols`. The client application will be able to recognize that row and column values of `-1` indicate that an environment is unbounded.

Each of the remaining lines in an environment `.dat` file represents an individual fish type, location, and direction in the environment. Such a line might look like Listing 7.19.

```
DarterFish 6 8 West
```

Listing 7.19 How a fish is represented in a `.dat` *file*

In order to extract fish information from a `.dat` file, we need to loop through each remaining line using a `for` loop. As with the first line, we store each line in a `String` and then use the `Split()` method to split it into a four-element array (`fishLineArray`). At the end of each loop iteration, we store the current `fishLineArray` as an element in an `ArrayList` named `fArrayList`. Add the code in Listing 7.20 to the `getEnv()` method.

```
String[] fishLineArray;
ArrayList fArrayList = new ArrayList();
for (String fishLine = reader. ReadLine();
    fishLine != null; fishLine = reader.ReadLine())
{
 fishLineArray = fishLine.Split(splitter.toCharArray());
 fArrayList.Add(fishLineArray);
}
```

Listing 7.20 Extracting fish information from a `.dat` *file*

The loop in Listing 7.20 ends when there are no more lines to read in the `.dat` file. At that point, `fArrayList` will contain a set of four-element arrays representing every fish in the environment. We convert `fArrayList` to an array (using the `.ToArray()` method) and assign it to the `myFishList` variable in `sEnv`. We then close the `StringReader` (`reader`) and `return` the completed `sEnv` to the client, ending the `getEnv()` method. Add the three lines in Listing 7.21 to `getEnv()`.

```
sEnv.myFishList = fArrayList.ToArray();
reader.Close();
return sEnv;
```

Listing 7.21 The final three lines of `getEnv()`

The getEnv() Web Method is complete. Test it by opening a browser and navigating to http://localhost/MBSEnvironmentService/ Environments.asmx. Click the **getEnv** link. Provide a value for envFileString, such as "C:\Program Files\MBS Case Study for Visual J# .NET\DataFiles\3species.dat," and then click the **Invoke** button. The getEnv() method should return an XML document like the one shown in Figure 7.10.

You can find complete, downloadable code for MBSEnvironmentService at JS070006.

Turning the MBS Application into a Web Service Client

As mentioned previously, the MBS Case Study itself will be the client for the Web Service we have just written. There are three major changes we need to make to the MBS code in order to give it the ability to access remote data files through MBSEnvironmentService.

1. We need to add a menu item to the GUI File menu to "Import Environment from the Web." Adding the menu item itself is easily accomplished via the Design window for GUIForm.jsl, but there is also a significant amount of code that must be added

Figure 7.10 Response from getEnv() *Web Method*

to the menu option's CodeBehind. The main purpose of this CodeBehind is to call the getFileList() Web Method and retrieve a list of available .dat files on the Web Service machine. We will display an additional form asking the user to select one of these files, and pass this file name to the method described in Step 2.

2. We need to add a method to the CodeBehind for GUIForm.jsl that is responsible for calling the getEnv() Web Method and retrieving a SerializableEnvironment for the file name obtained in Step 1. This method will be very similar to the existing method OpenFileAndPopulateData(), except that it will populate an environment with data from a remote Web Service rather than from a local file. Once a SerializableEnvironment is obtained, we use a special class called MBSSerializableEnvHandler (Step 3) to deserialize it and populate a GUI environment with the information it contains.

3. Finally, we need to create a new class, MBSSerializableEnvHandler, which will be used to create the local environment using the data obtained from the Web Service. MBSSerializableEnvHandler creates the Environment class used by the MBS GUI.

The three changes that must be made to the Marine Biology Simulation application are somewhat lengthy, and have therefore been relegated to the CodeNotes website. Please visit CodeNotes Pointer ⌖JS070008 to find detailed instructions on how to enable Web Service accessibility in the MBS.

BUGS AND CAVEATS

The Fish Must Be Available Locally
Although the Web Service will transfer the environment from a central source to a specific simulation, you still need to ensure that all of the fish types are available. For example, if the environment specifies HungryFish, but the client does not have a HungryFish type, then the environment will not be transferred correctly.

Chapter Summary

Microsoft's J# version of the Marine Biology Simulation Case Study is a complete conversion of the original Java language version into a Visual Studio .NET project. The Visual Studio .NET IDE allows you to modify both the MBS GUI and its CodeBehind in a visual environment, making it easy to add to and modify the existing application.

In this chapter, we looked at how to add a new fish (HungryFish) to the MBS Case Study, and how to make that fish available to the MBS Windows Form GUI. We also showed how fish and environment data can be made available over the Web by creating the MBSEnvironmentService Web Service, and how the MBS itself can be used as a Web Service client simply by importing a Web Reference (⟡JS070008).

You will find that being creative and making your own modifications and additions to the MBS Case Study is an excellent learning experience and will help you become accustomed to both the J# language and the .NET Framework. Although the smaller examples used throughout the rest of this book are very helpful for understanding particular concepts, a larger-scale application like the MBS Case Study will give you a good idea of what software development might be like in the real world.

Chapter 8

ADVANCED TOPICS

So far in the *CodeNotes for J#* we have looked at basic J# syntax (Chapter 3), Windows Forms (Chapter 4), ASP.NET (Chapter 5), and Web Services (Chapter 6). We have also examined the Marine Biology Case Study (Chapter 7), a larger application developed in J# that should give you an idea of just what is possible with J# and the .NET Framework. However, what you have seen in this book is only the beginning—the capabilities of J# and the .NET Framework extend far beyond the introduction that this book provides.

In this chapter, we're going to examine briefly some other major technologies available to .NET developers. These technologies include ADO.NET for database interaction, .NET Remoting for remote method calling, and cross-language inheritance. The benefits of these technologies will become readily apparent when you start developing more serious applications in J#.

Because this chapter is meant to provide a very brief introduction to some additional features, we will forgo the usual CodeNotes chapter format. That is, there will be no "Simple Application" or "Core Concepts," as each topic is fairly independent. In addition, you will find that the examples for each topic have been replaced by CodeNotes pointers.

Topic: Database Access

A database is a means of organizing related information into tables (with rows and columns). Relational databases (the most common kind) can contain multiple tables linked together by keys (a specific column shared by both tables). Databases are generally hosted by a database server, such as Microsoft SQL Server. Information is inserted into and extracted from databases using queries, which are usually constructed in Structured Query Language (SQL).

The .NET Framework contains classes that represent various aspects of database manipulation such as database connections, SQL commands, and sets of extracted data. In this topic, we will demonstrate how you can use these classes in your J# application in order to interact with a database. The Framework classes for database interaction are divided into two categories:

- ADO.NET classes represent database connections and SQL commands and can be used to interact programmatically with existing databases.
- Many Windows Forms controls and ASP.NET Web Controls can be *data-bound,* meaning that such controls can use a database table (or part of a table, or data from multiple tables) as a source for the information the control will contain. In addition to some controls with which you are already familiar from Chapter 4 (such as TextBox), there are controls designed specifically for displaying database data (such as DataGrid, which we will examine in this topic).

Although the Framework includes built-in classes for interacting with Microsoft SQL Server, Oracle, OLE (Object Linking and Embedding), and ODBC-accessible databases, you will be able to download APIs for most major databases and include them in your J# applications. If you are using a database other than the aforementioned, you will need to find a Managed Provider for that database in order to access it through the .NET Framework. We will look at Managed Providers in more detail in the ADO.NET section. If you're not familiar with the concept of a database or with SQL, you may want to see ⟨CN⟩JS080001 for a refresher before continuing with this topic.

ADO.NET

ADO.NET is Microsoft's new paradigm for accessing and manipulating databases. You will use databases to store relational data for many of your J# applications. A database provides a level of permanence to both online and offline applications, allowing you to persist information outside the runtime of the application. Using ADO.NET, you can communicate with any database by a paradigm that is specifically designed for distributed computing. The ADO.NET model is built primarily on the concepts of disconnected data islands (which will be explained in a moment). We will take a brief look at the ADO.NET Framework and demonstrate a brief example that displays data extracted from an SQL query.

Managed Providers

A Managed Provider is a set of classes designed to communicate with a particular type of database. If you have worked with databases in Java, a Managed Provider is similar in many ways to a JDBC Driver; however, there are numerous differences. The Managed Provider is responsible for communicating with the database in a language that the database understands. All Managed Providers fall under the `System.Data` namespace and support the following major classes:

- `Connection` An ADO.NET `Connection` is used to establish a connection to a database.
- `Command` A `Command` is used to execute SQL statements against the database.
- `DataReader` The `DataReader` is one method for storing the results of a database query. The `DataReader` is a highly optimized forward-only, read-only method to examine data.
- `Dataset` The `Dataset` is a more versatile mechanism for storing results of a database query. A `Dataset` is disconnected (meaning that it is independent of the rest of the data in the database), can be read in any direction, and can also be updated.
- `DataAdapter` A `DataAdapter` acts as the mediator between the Managed Provider and the disconnected `Dataset`. The `DataAdapter` translates the changes in a disconnected `Dataset` into SQL commands that can access and modify the database contents.

Although ADO.NET is designed to work with any database, you must select a Managed Provider that is designed specifically for your database system. The .NET Framework 1.1 ships with four optimized Managed Providers in the following namespaces:

- System.Data.Oledb   OLEDB Managed Provider for use with any database that supports OLE. This includes Oracle and SQL Server.
- System.Data.SqlClient   Managed Provider for SQL Server.
- System.Data.Odbc   Managed Provider for ODBC-accessible databases.
- System.Data.OracleClient   Managed Provider for Oracle databases. Note that you need to add a reference to the System.Data. OracleClient namespace to your application in order to use this Managed Provider.

For a list of other Managed Providers, see ⟳JS080002.

The Dataset

The Dataset object lies at the heart of ADO.NET. Using the DataAdapter object, you populate a Dataset with relevant data. The database is then closed, and all data is temporarily stored in the Dataset. Changes to the Dataset (inserts, updates, deletes) do not persist against the database, but are performed entirely in the Dataset's memory (hence the term *disconnected*). The only time the underlying database changes is when you use a DataAdapter explicitly in order to update the database based on the contents of your Dataset. The DataAdapter will read your Dataset and use the appropriate Managed Provider to force the required modifications to the given database.

A Dataset is an in-memory representation of a database. An ADO.NET Dataset can contain multiple tables from a database and the relationships among them. In addition, the Dataset can enforce relational constraints on the data it contains. Thus it is better to think of the Dataset as a lightweight in-memory database.

DATA–BOUND CONTROLS

Data-bound controls are Windows Forms controls or Web Controls that can be bound to a data source. Data-bound controls are typically used to display information extracted from a database in a user-readable format. The most commonly used control for displaying database information is a DataGrid control. DataGrid can be found in the Visual Studio .NET toolbox under Windows Forms. Figure 8.1 shows a DataGrid control displaying some information extracted from a database.

You can use two different mechanisms to populate a DataGrid with information extracted from a database.

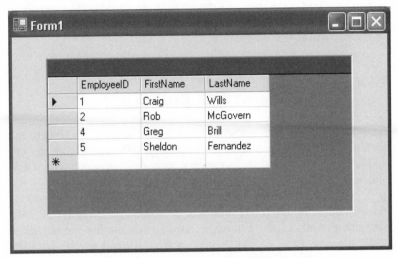

Figure 8.1 A DataGrid control displaying some data

- **Programmatically** You can write code to create a connection to the database, execute a SQL statement to retrieve some information into a Dataset, and then assign that Dataset as the data source for the DataGrid by using a line of code like Listing 8.1.

```
dataGrid1.set_DataSource(myDataSet.get_Tables().get_Item(0));
```

Listing 8.1 Setting the DataSource for a DataGrid control

We will demonstrate the complete code for this approach in the example at ◦CN◦JS080003.

- **Visually** An alternative is to use the controls found in the Data section of the VS .NET toolbox. These controls can be dragged and dropped into the Design window of an application and will automatically allow you to create a "data source" by using a built-in wizard. Once you set up a data source, you can assign it to any data-bound control by setting the control's DataSource property. You can find an example of visually populating a Data-Grid at ◦CN◦JS080004.

Many other controls found in the VS .NET toolbox can also be assigned a DataSource, including ListBox, CheckedListBox, and ComboBox. See ◦CN◦JS080005 for a complete list of data-bound controls.

You can find a complete example of using data-bound controls in combination with ADO.NET classes (including a sample downloadable OLE database) at ⌀ JS080006.

Topic: .NET Remoting

.NET Remoting enables a client on one machine to access objects and methods on another machine. Conceptually, .NET Remoting is very similar to the Web Services framework, as both allow you to communicate with a remote object. The difference is the amount of flexibility at the hands of the developer. Whereas Web Services stipulate that objects must reside in the IIS server and must communicate using HTTP, software components exposed through Remoting do not have to be placed under the scrutiny of a Web Server such as IIS and can be accessed through fast communication protocols such as TCP/IP.

The added flexibility of Remoting, however, comes at the cost of complexity and limitation. In addition to working through company firewall issues, developing a .NET Remoting solution can also take you into the fairly difficult concepts of channels, object lifetime, and leasing.

PROXIES

.NET Remoting is based on the concept of a proxy object. When a client application uses a remote object (one on a different machine), it does not talk directly with the component. Instead, it talks to a proxy object, which ferries calls to the real object. Through this illusion, the proxy acts as a mediator between client and server, encapsulating all of the logic required to package and transmit messages between the two entities.

The manner in which a proxy communicates to its remote counterpart is based on two concepts: a *channel* and a *formatter.* A channel determines the communication protocol by which method invocations are transmitted across machines. Developers can choose from the following communication protocols supported by the .NET Framework:

- **HTTP**   Similar to Web Services. Messages between client and server proceed as standard HTTP. HTTP is good for cases when a firewall separates the client from the server.
- **TCP**   In cases where opening new ports on a firewall is not a concern, the TCP channel offers greater performance.

Whereas a channel prescribes how messages are sent between proxy and remote objects, a formatter determines the representation of the messages. The .NET Framework provides two formatters: the BinaryFormatter, in which messages are stored in a binary byte representation, and the SoapFormatter class, which translates messages into user-friendly XML (you should recall SOAP from Chapter 6 of this CodeNote).

By default, the HTTP channel uses the SOAP formatter to encode and decode messages to and from the remote object. The higher-performance TCP channel, on the other hand, uses the Binary formatter by default. Note that the .NET Remoting is designed in an extensible way in order to allow third parties to customize or design their own channels and formatters. Information on extending the Remoting infrastructure can be found in the MSDN.

REMOTING

Recall that Web Service components do not maintain state in between method invocations. Each time a client calls the Web Service, the Web Service class is instantiated, used, and destroyed. .NET Remoting is more versatile. Depending upon your requirements, a remote object can be configured in one of three ways:

1. **Single Call**   The remote object is instantiated for the sole purpose of responding to one request (from one specific client), after which the object is deallocated (i.e., destroyed).
2. **Singleton**   The remote object is instantiated to server requests from various clients.
3. **Client Activated Objects**   As the name suggests, this remote object is instantiated upon request from a client. Client Activated Objects remain dedicated to one specific client.

Configuring a remote object as a *Single Call* object makes sense when the object is required by a client to do a certain amount of work, after which the object is no longer required. For example, a *Single Call* object may calculate and return an interest rate. A *Singleton* object, on the other hand, is used in cases where multiple clients speak with the same remote object and share data among one another. A *Singleton* server object may, for example, serve as a chat engine. Finally, *Client Activated Objects* serve well when a single client needs access to the remote object, but repeatedly calls methods on the object. In this case, keeping the remote object alive for several requests reduces the overhead associated with component instantiation.

HOSTING A REMOTE OBJECT

Once you have decided the configuration of a remote object (Single Call or Singleton versus Client Activated), as well as the communication channel to be used, the next step is to host the remote object on a server. Recall that Web Services are hosted by IIS. When a SOAP request arrives for a service, IIS takes care of instantiating and directing method calls to the proper .NET component. Remoting components can also be hosted in IIS. On machines without IIS, however, you can also host a remote object in a standard .NET executable. You can find an example of how to create, host, and call a remote object at ☜JS080007.

Topic: Cross-Language Inheritance

Because all .NET languages are compiled to Microsoft Intermediate Language (MSIL), classes written in .NET languages are capable of cross-language inheritance with few limitations. This means that a class written in J# could be inherited by a class written in C# or VB.NET.

The potential for cross-language inheritance comes as the result of .NET architecture. All managed languages target MSIL. This targeting results in code that is actually compiled twice: once to MSIL when you compile your application and once more from MSIL to the underlying OS's native set of instructions when the application is actually run.

There are some restrictions on cross-language inheritance, which result from differences in the syntax and capabilities of the high-level programming languages built on top of MSIL (J#, C#, etc.). Most languages implement a "selected features set" of MSIL, in that not all MSIL code can be produced from any given language. For example, as mentioned in Chapter 3, J# does not allow you to define your own value types or events, because the Java language syntax on which J# is based does not have that functionality. Therefore, inheritance between two languages is possible only if the inherited code contains only features available in both of those languages.

For example, it is not possible to define new operators in J#; that is, you can't override the functionality of the + or * operators. C#, however, does allow definition and overloading of operators. Therefore, a J# class cannot inherit from a C# class that defines operators. It is important to keep in mind the restrictions of various languages when you are developing applications in multiple languages.

For an example of cross-language inheritance using J#, please see ☜JS080008.

Chapter Summary

Throughout *CodeNotes for J#,* we have tried to provide you with the most thorough introduction possible to the potential of J# and the .NET Framework. Nevertheless, this book is only the beginning of the story. There are many more .NET technologies, such as Attributes and Reflection, which are beyond the scope of this book. Your best sources of information if you plan to research further into .NET technologies (whether or not they are covered in this book) are:

- The CodeNotes website (www.codenotes.com), on which you can use our search engine to find articles on many .NET Framework topics (including those covered by other books in the CodeNotes series)
- The Microsoft Developer Network (MSDN, http://msdn.microsoft.com), a complete reference to every namespace, class, and method in the .NET Framework. If you find a term with which you are not familiar or a method whose functionality you need to determine, MSDN is the first place you should look.

Index